Contents

OPEN AND DISTANCE LEARNING SERIES

E-moderating: The Key to Teaching and Learning Online

GILLY SALMON

KOGAN PAGE

London • Sterling (USA)

For Emily

First published in 2000
Reprinted 2000

Apart from any fair dealing for the purposes of research or private study, or criticism or review, as permitted under the Copyright, Designs and Patents Act 1988, this publication may only be reproduced, stored or transmitted, in any form or by any means, with the prior permission in writing of the publishers, or in the case of reprographic reproduction in accordance with the terms and licences issued by the CLA. Enquiries concerning reproduction outside these terms should be sent to the publishers at the undermentioned address:

Kogan Page Limited
120 Pentonville Road
London N1 9JN
UK

Stylus Publishing
22883 Quicksilver Drive
Sterling VA 20166-2012
USA

British Library Cataloguing in Publication Data

A CIP record for this book is available from the British Library.

ISBN 0 7494 3110 5

Typeset by JS Typesetting, Wellingborough, Northants
Printed and bound in Great Britain by Clays Ltd, St Ives plc

Series editor's foreword

The last ten years have seen an amazing growth in the number of resources and activities, events and courses available online. This growth is not only likely to continue but to accelerate as major telecommunications, business, leisure and education institutions join forces. It is now common place to book a flight or a theatre ticket, to buy your groceries or even a car online via the World Wide Web. Via the Web you can browse virtual bookshelves and order a book, take part in a virtual seminar and contribute to an online academic journal. From your desk you can take part in an intranet company training programme or be part of a worldwide group following a degree course with a university thousands of miles from where you are living – and with colleagues you may never meet.

The revolution in Communication and Information Technology has had a profound impact upon teaching and learning. The change is from a model based upon the transmission of knowledge, from teacher to learner, to its construction within a learning community; from exposition to facilitation. This change is being achieved by a new generation of teachers and trainers that Gilly Salmon describes as 'e-moderators' – those who work with learners online in an electronic environment. At the moment many of these enthusiasts, *early adopters*, are operating by intuition. However, in *E-moderating: the key to teaching and learning online*, Gilly Salmon draws upon her own research and her considerable experience not only as an e-moderator but as a trainer of e-moderators over several years. Through numerous examples and illustrations, she explains the qualities and competencies that such e-moderators will need and how training can be provided. She compares the experience of both learners and e-moderators and the support that they need. The book also offers a unique collection of Resources for Practitioners, comprising advice and guidelines on subjects from Choosing a software system for Computer Mediated Conferencing (CMC) to Monitoring e-moderating. These will be invaluable to those of us facing the challenge of teaching online.

A major contribution to our thinking is the five-stage model which Gilly Salmon offers that describes the progress of learners as they move from being a novice to being competent, progressing through the stages of Access and motivation, to Online socialization, Information exchange and Knowledge construction and eventually to Development. I wish I had been aware of this model, and its significance, before I became an e-moderator on a Web-based degree course in 1999. My sensitivity to learner needs, to the roles open to me and to the development of the learners would have been enhanced. It is not too late for us. I hope you enjoy this book, find it insightful and that both you and your learners benefit.

Fred Lockwood
February 2000

Preface

E-moderators are the new generation of teachers and trainers who work with learners online. I hope this book will 'strike a spark' and help make the online world a creative, happy, productive and relevant place for successful learning.

Human use of computing is vast and growing. Networked technologies such as the Internet and the World Wide Web have been called 'transformational' because of their wide-ranging impact. Electronic networking creates communications across terrestrial boundaries, across cultures and on a global scale. Concepts of space and time are changing, and of how and with whom people can collaborate, discover communities, explore resources and ideas and learn.

Computer Mediated Communication and its collaborative sister, Computer Mediated Conferencing (CMC), actually arrived before the Internet and the World Wide Web became widely available. CMC has encouraged teachers to challenge perceived and received wisdom and practice about learning online and to reflect on their experiences. In this book I call attention to the mediator, or e-moderator, in online learning processes. Successful online learning depends on teachers and trainers acquiring new competencies, on their becoming aware of its potential and on their inspiring the learners, rather than on mastering the technology.

Investigating the use of CMC has many facets and aspects. Web utopians are predicting virtual universities with very low cost learning and truly effective 'any time, any place' student interaction. They say that the need for expensive campus buildings or large corporate training facilities will disappear along with the requirement for learners to physically congregate. The 'Web-phobes' are very worried that the benefits of learning together may be lost and that it will be a bad day for knowledge, for feelings, for the joys of gatherings and groups.

Meanwhile, some of us are getting on with it! Small factions of teachers, researchers and trainers have led the way. Like all pioneers, they have a tough time. For them, and for the thousands of online teachers that will follow, I hope this book will be of interest and of use. It's time to start the wagon train again but this time with a rough and ready trail to follow!

There are many definitions of an online course. At one end of the spectrum of 'online-ness', these include classroom-based teaching supplemented by lecture notes posted on a Web site or by electronic communication such as e-mail. At the other end of the spectrum, materials may be made available and interactions occur exclusively through networked technologies. This book is concerned with more or less the full spectrum (and not-yet-created combinations), but the key issue is that the teacher, instructor, tutor or facilitator – the e-moderator – is operating in the electronic environment along with his or her students, the participants.

I have drawn on my own experience of Computer Mediated Conferencing, as well as that of many other people. I have selected case studies and experiences where the storyteller is the academic, teacher or e-moderator involved, where implementation occurred within the regular training or teaching situation, and where there was some evaluation or at least serious reflection on practice.

For some years, I have been able to study and practise the art of e-moderating, particularly within the Open University (OU). I began learning online in 1988, when I was a student on the first OU course to use CMC on a large scale. The software and systems we had at that time were primitive, although they felt revolutionary to me! I was excited by the experience and by CMC's potential. In 1988, we used a system called 'CoSy' (short for Conferencing System) that worked on commands from the keyboard. Offline readers, point and click mouse commands, graphics and ever increasing sophistication of functions followed as software systems developed. Each new function seemed like a great step forward at the time. When I joined the OU Business School (OUBS) as a lecturer in 1989, I was able to experiment with CMC for teaching management courses at a distance. In the last few years I have been responsible for training hundreds of e-moderators for the School.

You will appreciate the irony of writing a book about something I strongly believe needs to be experienced in the electronic environment itself. So while I have been putting the book together, I have thought of you, the readers, as potential collaborators in an online experience. I think of you as:

- academics, teachers, course managers, teaching assistants, tutors, instructors, moderators and trainers of any discipline at post-secondary level in any country or training department, who are planning to move from conventional teaching to teaching online or who are working in open and distance learning;
- developers of 'corporate universities', training departments of large companies, brokers of and agents for online training.

I believe there may be some 'lurkers' or 'browsers', too. They are likely to be:

- software designers who are working on education and training projects;
- developers considering the use of CMC in educational programmes;
- teachers working in primary and secondary schools;
- staff in community programmes or local government departments dealing with health and social welfare who are planning to use CMC for building communities or for democratic purposes;

- managers and academics responsible for assessment of trainees' and teachers' performance.

In Part 1, Chapter 1 explains what I see as e-moderating and explores it. The next chapter offers a research-based model for understanding training and development for CMC. Chapter 3 explores the roles and competencies of e-moderators, with examples. Chapter 4 explores the key issues in training e-moderators and Chapter 5 looks at the learners' experiences. No book of this kind, with the use of CMC in its infancy, can resist a peek at the future, which you'll find in Chapter 6.

Part 2 of the book changes tack and offers a set of practical resources based largely on my own practice as an e-moderator and e-trainer. I hope you will find them useful for meeting this exciting challenge.

This book will provide you with support in thinking through your online teaching, for your topic, your subject, your organization, your programme, your teaching practice and your learners. This is the way to take part and *shape* the future of teaching and learning online – through the actions of the e-moderators.

Gilly Salmon
Epping Forest
February 2000

Acknowledgements

This book has been touched by the experience of many different people, mainly through their keyboards. David Hawkridge's patient exploration, critique and insightful comments throughout the book's development have been incredibly valuable to me. My colleague in the Open University Business School, Ken Giles, is always supportive and creative online and offline and has tracked the research and the book's progress from beginning to end with full encouragement.

My thanks go to case study contributors, who shared their online experience with me: Haydn Blackey, Tony Fiddes, David Hawkridge, Marie-Noëlle Lamy, Sandra Luxton, Gerry Prendergast, and Claudine SchWeber. And thanks too to all of their online participants – a cast of thousands!

Many others offered me inspiration, suggestions, comments, sources, help and experiences and encouragement: Gary Alexander, Anne Armstrong, Edis Bevan, Carol Daunt, Margaret Debenham, Roger Dence, Tom Kernan, Jan Kingsley, Robin Mason, Bob Masterton, Norman Maxfield, Patricia McCarthy, Dave Mcara, Caroline Middleton, Grant Miller, David Murphy, Peter Neal, Emir O'Healy, Daxa Patel, Anita Pincas, Jenny Preece, Andrew Remely, Sally Reynolds, John Scully, David Shepherd, Cynthia Sherwood, Dale Spender, Robin Stenham, Denis Tocher, Jo Wackrill and Jazz Webb.

Chapter 6, The key to the future, is an exploration of a variety of views from those with special insight. Many thanks to all who gave generously of their time and thoughts to talk to me: Drs Michal Beller and Ehud Or of the Open University in Israel; Dr Zane Berge of the University of Maryland, Baltimore County; Dr Joanna Bull of the Computer Assisted Assessment Centre at Luton University; Sir John Daniel, Vice-Chancellor of the Open University; Professor Marc Eisenstadt of OU's Knowledge Media Institute; Charles Jennings of Network Knowledge Architechs Ltd; Gary Maitkin of University of California at Berkeley; Professor Jean-Louis Michelet of International Cyber University Singapore; Professor Tim O'Shea, Master of Birkbeck College, London; Dr Andy DiPaolo, Exec. Director, Stanford Center for Professional Development; Vicky Seehusen of Colorado Electronic Community College; Dr Mary Beth Susman, Chief Executive of Kentucky Commonwealth Virtual University; Steve Tilson, Director of the Technology-Based Learning Center, Front Range Community College, Westminster, Colorado, and Bob Threlkeld of CSU Fresno, California.

I am also grateful to the developers of FirstClass software, MC2 Learning Systems/SoftArc Inc of Toronto for permission to show screen shots using FirstClass software.

Some 400 or so Associate Lecturers from the Business School ploughed through the online training and then e-moderated for real. Many of the checklists in Part 2 are based on their experiences and feedback. I hope their online 'voices' shine through. Many of them I've got to know very well online over the years, but have never met.

Thanks to my partner, Rod Angood, my sister Jackie Bocchiola for critical reading and meals and my (grown-up-networked) children, Glenn, Emily and Paula for loving support and encouragement.

Finally, I thank my faculty, the Open University Business School, for the brilliant opportunities to work online and for some leave to think and write away from the everyday excitement.

Part 1: CONCEPTS AND CASES

Chapter 1

What is e-moderating?

This book is set in the context of the rapid development of Information and Communication Technology (ICT). Its key focus and emphasis is on the changes to learning made possible by ICT, but I look at these changes through the eyes of online teachers, for whom I have used the term 'electronic moderators' – 'e-moderators'. This chapter introduces e-moderating to you and explores the contexts and environments in which it thrives.

The term 'online' came from the days of the telegraph, when messages could be tapped directly onto the line rather than prepared 'offline' on perforated tape, for sending when the machine was connected later to the telephone line. Today, 'online' covers a range of technologies. In education and training, technologies that concentrate on computer mediated communication are commonest. They fall into three broad categories as defined by Santoro (1995):

1. Informatics, particularly involving electronic access via telecommunications to catalogues, library resources, interactive remote databases and archives, including those on the World Wide Web.
2. Computer-assisted instruction, also known as computer-assisted learning and computer-based training, which may or may not require telecommunications.
3. Computer-mediated conferencing, which is the medium, based on computers and telecommunications, that is explored throughout this book and within which e-moderators do much of their work with students.

A moderator is a person who presides over a meeting. An e-moderator presides over an electronic online meeting or conference, though not in quite the same ways as a moderator does. Computer-mediated conferencing (CMC) actually requires e-moderators to have a rather wider range of expertise, as I shall explain and demonstrate.

Jane's diary

Here are a few pages from Jane's diary. She's an e-moderator, and it will give you the flavour of what this job can be like. Jane is a university teacher, like me, and she's an enthusiast too.

Day 1, Thursday, 10 pm

Just back from swimming. I check my course list: 16 students this time, from four continents. I hope they've all received the first mailing in the post, including their log-on instructions and my first requests. I try not to plead too hard for them to get started really early on the conferencing!

How many will have logged in by Day 1? I click on the Cross-cultural Management conference icon. Then into the 'Arrivals' thread. And there it is on my screen! The 'new message' flag. The conferencing begins! It's great getting to know new students. Abraham is confident:

> Hi there.
>
> ABRAHAM HAS LIFT OFF! OR IS IT LANDING?
> I'VE ARRIVED IN THIS INTERESTING NEW PLACE AND I'M READY TO BEGIN.
> Who can tell me what's what around here?

This one's perhaps timid:

> I hope I'm posting this message in the right place. Can someone tell me?
> Marianne from Manchester

Out of my 16, 8 have got there so far and have announced their arrival, as I asked them to. Another two have e-mailed me. Paula in Moscow says she's having connection problems. Ben can't find the Cross-cultural Management conference icon on his screen. I e-mailed both back with ways of contacting technical support and diaried myself to follow up in a few days.

So, I e-mail the arrivals to thank and encourage them for their first conference messages. I mention to Abraham that capital letters are equivalent to shouting online. I check the message history for the arrivals conference – two more have been reading the messages but haven't contributed yet. I'm sure they will soon. I make that 12 on the runway.

I check the conference for their second task: to use the 'resume' facility to tell the group a little about themselves. Time online: 45 minutes.

Day 3, Saturday, 10.45 am

Super! Two more in arrivals, one from Beijing, one from London. Fourteen on the runway now. Some chat occurring in arrivals between those already there. I need to archive to avoid too many unread messages (especially as 6 were from Abraham) for the final arrival I post a message asking people to move across to the café conference and put a couple of chatty messages in there myself. Time online: 15 minutes.

Day 5, Monday, 10 pm

Out for a pizza then log on. Fifteen chatty messages in café conference and one more new arrival – Sylvia from Vienna.

Set first conference for carrying out course activities. As a 'warm-up' activity, I post this message:

> Task 1 Over the next few days, visit a local store that sells soft drinks. Try and find the cheapest of the kind on offer of:
>
> Coca Cola
> Local cola brand.
>
> Check out how each type of cola is priced, the place where you found it and the type of promotion it was being given. Please give price per can or bottle.
> Then convert your currency into sterling through a currency converter Web site.
> Post your results in this conference by next Sunday 7 pm GMT.
> Abraham and Marianne have agreed to collate and post comparative results.
> As an example, I went to my local supermarket in Loughton in North East London in the United Kingdom.
> Here are my results:
>
> Price for Coca-Cola: £0.38, ie 38p (but sold only in packs of 6 for £2.25)
> Price for local cola: Safeways 'Select' Cola £0.28 (but sold only in packs of 6 cans for £1.69)
> Promotion for Coca-Cola: displayed at eye level on soft drinks shelf (Pepsi Cola was below eye level)
> Promotion for local cola: displayed at eye level along with options, e.g. caffeine-free. The packaging and colour very similar to Coca-Cola.

Time online: 10 minutes.

Day 10, Saturday, 6.45 am

Going out for the day so I log on early.

The facilitators for the cola activity, Abraham and Marianne, report by e-mail that they have 13 results in. They are chasing the other two.

Check message histories throughout the conference. I'm still one participant completely missing online. Check participants' list, this is a Philip Brown from Dublin. Time online: 10 minutes.

Phone technical helpline. They've had no requests for help from P. Brown. Fax him to ask what problems?

Day 13, Tuesday, 7.15 am

Log on before leaving for work.

Marianne has posted a spreadsheet giving 15 results (14 from students plus mine) for the 'cola' exercise. I set up a sub-conference with starter questions:

What do the results tell you about the way soft drinks are marketed in your home location, compared to the others? What do they tell you about:

1. The economy of your location?
2. The habits of cola drinking throughout the world? Are there any indications of cultural differences?
3. Your views on the nature of global brands?

Time online: 5 minutes.

Day 18, Sunday, 7.30 pm

Log on quickly while the family are clearing up the garden after a barbecue.

E-mail from the course administrator that P. Brown from Dublin has dropped out of the course due to connection problems. Very annoying, wonder if it's recoverable? I will compose a snail-mail letter to him.

The cola exchange sub-conference has really taken off. There are 36 messages in it. I do a quick analysis:

4 people had posted 1 message each;
3 people had posted 5 messages;
4 people had posted 2 messages;
3 people had posted 3 messages;
1 reading everything but not contributing.

I summarize the relevant contributions into one 'key points' message and archive the originals so participants can access them if they like. Two people – Anton and Jeremy – had started a conversation in the cola conference about alcohol and their local driving laws. I archive these messages with the rest but e-mail A. and J. to suggest they continue this conversation by e-mail. Time online: 35 minutes.

Day 20, Tuesday, 12.30 pm

Log on from the office in my lunch break to set up the first assignment.

I divide the 'class' into two groups for this exercise – one group of 8 and one of 7. I mix up activists and reflectors in the groups, based on my experience of them so far. Post URL with notes on forming virtual teams and online collaboration. Appoint facilitators for each team, and e-mailed them basic e-moderating points to help them

Make as clear as I can the requirements for assessment and deadlines for submission. Time online: 35 minutes.

Day 30, Friday, 4 pm

Log on from office and look in on Assignment 1 discussions.

Team A have built themselves a clear objectives and a triple conference structure for their team. They've spent the first few days in dividing up tasks and responsibilities. In Conference 1 'Data', the student facilitator has asked each participant to post a set of data about themselves. In Conference 2 'Concepts', Peter's summarized the data in Conference 1, and put his views on how this relates to Hofstede and there is the start of a discussion. Conference 3 'Meanings?', is currently empty except for its introduction message, saying this is the place for developing the written assignment!

Team B has started with just one conference, where they introduced themselves, explained their backgrounds, education, families, interests and the places they had lived in the world. People seem to be enjoying explaining about themselves and only two messages have gone over the suggested 'one screenful' in length. There are several interesting threads, where participants are finding their similarities and differences. No leader has emerged yet but two participants appear to be taking responsibility for progressing the discussions, while another is complaining about the two who are reading but not posting messages – saying this is not 'fair'. I'll wait for a few more days to see if they start putting some structure into this before intervening.

I post a message in our 'information' conference to say I'll be away for three days and offline. Time online: 20 minutes.

E-moderating, a new way of teaching

E-moderating along the lines of Jane's conference, is becoming a new way of teaching, particularly in higher education. The rest of this chapter examines the context of e-moderating.

The availability of networked computers in homes and at work is rapidly increasing, while costs to CMC users are falling, making conferences like this one accessible to large numbers of participants. CMC raises extremely challenging issues for education, however, including complex partnerships, funding, intellectual property. Most of all, CMC calls for the training and development of new kinds of online teachers – the e-moderators of this book – to carry out roles not yet widely understood.

As the Internet and the World Wide Web have expanded, opportunities to use it for teaching and learning have expanded too – some people call this 'networked learning'. Educationists all over the world are experimenting with various forms of distance, open and flexible learning. Networked computing offers the chance to build a learning community: this can be in a university or college, in an industrial or commercial setting, or based on common interests or objectives rather than geographical location. I have met many academics and trainers who are very keen indeed to adopt these new ways to enliven teaching and learning in their subjects. Their institutions and organizations are investing heavily in technological systems, thus creating conditions in which networked learning can be widely available.

Monash University case study

Monash University in Australia was one of the first in the world to explore and exploit CMC for learning, and to take seriously the training of academic staff and e-moderators. They are still exploring the potential. Sandra Luxton, Lecturer and Co-ordinator of Undergraduate Open Learning in Marketing, describes her experiences.

> The current online curriculum at Monash closely reflects the content of the face-to-face and text-based distance education versions and uses a full range of media and computer technologies including the Internet, e-mail, bulletin boards, online library facilities, video, animations and hypertext. All subject content is provided via a Web site and all communication, including assignment submission, takes place via the Internet. The progression from print and on-campus materials to online has involved discontinuous innovation in that students' experience and learning are different online. Instructional design has been aimed at accommodating the differences.
>
> E-moderating Marketing Theory and Practice Online (MTPO) is a challenging, exciting task due to the very diverse student group this core business course serves. MTPO is offered to students taking various business studies majors on-campus, by distance education and through open learning, which is an unrestricted access option. Students vary in age, language and ethnic background. The e-moderator needs to help all of them to participate fruitfully on the bulletin boards. It is here that the anonymity of electronic learning is both an asset and a hindrance. Recent research based on students' diary records of their thoughts and experiences, shows that some enjoy being 'faceless' and are happy to contribute to discussions, but that others just cannot bring themselves to participate. Overcoming this paradox is a key task for the e-moderator, using varied strategies. To assist learners to find

their confidence in communicating online on unfamiliar topics, e-moderators increase online 'comfort' by starting informal and non-confronting discussion, and by using existing dialogue to prompt the next communication with another question. They also establish very simple dialogue in week 1 by asking students just to say 'hi', or answer yes/no questions. They try to alleviate some of the students' concerns by talking to them about what to expect.

E-moderators receive an operational and instructional guide, for both the content development and expectations for online e-modera-tion. This helps to ensure quality and consistency of delivery. However, within this educational framework, students digest and respond to the learning process differently. Asynchronous discussion gives them time to contemplate issues before adding their own contribution. Those with English as a second language, or who need to review terminology, or who have a full-time job, are less disadvantaged than in class. The e-moderator needs to be sympathetic and at all times supportive and encouraging, just as in a face-to-face class. Our students can get up to 5 per cent added to their final grade if they participate well on the bulletin board.

To encourage students to communicate with each other the e-moderator posts weekly discussion topics, that are not too 'daunting', written in a familiar way. Here is an example.

Week 1 discussion: what is marketing?

E-moderator:

This sounds like a strange question I guess, but it is one of the most common questions on exam papers! Is marketing really just about advertising?

Student C:

To be perfectly honest, my first thought of marketing was that it was advertising, sales, graphs and people doing presentations. The first time I realized that marketing was a whole lot more, was when three of my best friends finished their marketing degrees, and started their full time jobs in marketing with big firms... When we are out, the topic of conversation is always what we are doing at work, and every time we talk, I realize that marketing is a lot more than I first thought... but this was my first impression on marketing. I hope I have started the conversation on the right foot and I look forward to seeing other people's opinions. Talk to you all again soon.

Student H:

I was also fascinated to learn about the broad application marketing has within an organization. My dealings with the Marketing department, in the organization I used to work for, were mainly with regard to setting budgets (when I was in Administration) and trying to keep them from making outrageous or unsubstantiated claims about our products (when I was in Compliance). I found marketing people to generally be very creative with a lot of flair and 'get up and go' and not necessarily to be particularly sympathetic to budgetary or legislative constraints. In my experience they have not always worked well with other, less entrepreneurial parts of the organization. . . Although customer focus was touted around the organization, the main focus of our marketing appears to have been market positioning both in Australia and overseas, something I believe the organization is doing very effectively.

E-moderator:

Great comments! So often marketing is thought of as nothing more than advertising and selling – but it's about much more, as you rightly say! Hopefully this will be clear from reading your textbook as well. Your comments about large vs. small companies are very true. . . What is most critical, for any organization is. . . You will see through your reading that these are the firms most likely to be put up as exemplary. . . Do you think the role of marketing has changed much in recent years? Why?
Cheers

Because our online students have no face-to-face or telephone contact, the e-moderator also needs to ensure that they feel part of a 'class', and that their problems and concerns do not occur in isolation. We manage this by enabling students to 'workshop' some of the queries about assignments as a group, so that by exchanging ideas and opinions they develop a better understanding of the task at hand. For example, here is a discussion about an assignment.

E-moderator:

A recent question which others may like an answer to: I assume by 'business orientation' you mean which marketing philosophy the companies subscribe to. . . eg product, production, societal, etc. Is this correct?

> **Student B:**
>
> Isn't each philosophy (product and selling, etc) a different way that a company can conduct business, and one of these is a 'marketing philosophy or orientation?
>
> **Student M:**
>
> I've assumed that all the orientations described in Chapter 1 are different forms of marketing approaches, but I'm not totally sure.
>
> **E-moderator:**
>
> This is something that many students find a little confusing. Yes, a business philosophy is the approach that a firm takes in its business operations. One of the alternative approaches that may be adopted is a 'marketing orientation'. . . To clarify this further, can any of you think of an example of a firm for each of the business orientations?

At Monash, with good e-moderating, CMC is an effective approach to providing quality education to a diverse target market.

Teaching and learning online

The most optimistic commentators see a whole new world for learning:

> Every learner can, at his or her own choice of time and place, access a world of multimedia material. . . immediately the learner is unlocked from the shackles of fixed and rigid schedules, from physical limitations. . . and is released into an information world which reacts to his or her own pace of learning.
>
> (Benjamin, 1994: 49)

This renaissance view of teaching and learning is not universally shared, however, nor is it based on the record of what has been implemented to date. Millions of words have been written about the technology and its potential, but not much about what the teachers and learners actually do online.

Thousands of online discussion groups have started up among people with shared interests (Preece, 2000). Some prosper, others wither. Many change and grow with very little structure and no one person providing direction. Networked computers can provide vehicles for learning materials and interaction but students still need the 'champions' who make the learning come alive – the e-moderators.

Education and training are always undertaken for a purpose. Unlike casual browsing or playing computer games on the Web, a key distinction of online education and training is that they are very purposeful. Like their classmates on campus, students online need goals, usually ones provided by their teachers. Like their colleagues on campus, the e-moderators have to think through the design of structured learning experiences for their students. To exploit CMC for teaching, they must understand its potential, which is different from that of any other teaching medium.

At the Open University, with its well-established distance learning methodologies, most courses include some face-to-face sessions and do not yet include CMC. Some courses have a small proportion of online working based on e-mails only. Others have a Web site with online exercises and study guides. A few courses, ranging from small to extremely large in student numbers (from 35 to 10,000), include no face-to-face meetings and provide a good deal of teaching through CMC. In all OU courses, the students are never 'left on their own' with no support, direction or leadership. In courses with CMC this is where the e-moderator comes in!

Open University Business School in Wales case study

Haydn Blackey is an Associate Lecturer with the Open University Business School in Wales. He describes using CMC for analysing case studies. Haydn highlights the importance of transferring to CMC what we know about the dynamics of small face-to-face learning groups.

> B820 is an MBA course on business strategy that puts much emphasis on developing students' case study skills, which are normally reinforced in face-to-face meetings. For two successive groups, I developed practice sessions online for strategy case study analysis.
>
> For the first group, I used a short printed case (Case 1) but focused on students sharing their understanding and developing their analysis through online conferencing. I laid out a clear timetable at the beginning, with start and finish dates for each activity:

Week	Activity
1	Analysis of the context of the case and exploration of the key issues
2	Where are they now? (Developing SWOT, STEP and resources and capabilities analyses)
3	Where would they like to be? (Stakeholders, option development, option analysis, and option selection)
4	How are they going to get there? (Strategic selection)

As e-moderator, I was most active in weeks 1 and 2, when students were exploring which models might be used to undertake the analysis. My main roles were as group facilitator, developer and content provider. My first message suggested an approach to make best use of the conference. I set the conditions of the conference and the element of trust students should expect from each other in sharing ideas.

The work in weeks 1 and 2 was structured. I acted as adviser to the students in their exploration of the use of models. In weeks three and 4, when judgement was more important than model identification, I withdrew from active conference participation. By this time, the students' commitment to each other and the work they were doing became taken for granted and the conference became more reflective. They did not then need me to act as the 'expert'.

Four participants proved better at resource investigation than critical thinking. They used the course books and suggested models and concepts useful for the case analysis. Their approach was useful in the first two weeks of the conference. It appears that these students felt comfortable enough with the material in formal ways, but were less willing to take the risk of sharing their own ideas and interpretation.

Some students did not feel they could contribute, although these same students contributed in a face-to-face group. Perhaps they were unwilling to 'take a risk' with their ideas in a written form online than with a spoken non-stored medium? Of course, the ability to go back, delete or alter messages can help make participants feel that their mistakes are not going to be a long-term source of embarrassment. The e-moderator needs to be aware of the potential for embarrassment and allow for such deletions in the initial conference arrangements.

Watching the case study conference develop was fascinating, I could see how ideas were developed, reinforced, revisited and reformed. The CMC environment offered as good, perhaps a better, learning environment than a face-to-face tutorial. This was because students read messages, went away and thought about the issues and ideas, and came back the next day with a reflective and thought out comment. Such a process isn't possible in a face-to-face meeting.

After this initial success I used a similar approach with another group of B820 students, with Case 2. This time there were seven potential students: six participated fully. They had either failed or marginally passed their first assessment. Therefore, I used Case 2 as remedial support for learning about strategy. Case 1 went to the students as hard copy, but for Case 2 I generated and collated material about the automotive industry and delivered it online through the conference in timed chunks. Again I used weekly periods for debate:

Week	Activity
1	Discussion of the case – two companies before a merger
2	The merger – who were the winners and losers?
3	Who got it wrong?
4	Where next for the company?

This group of students had worked together online in preparing their first assignment, so the socialization elements of conferencing had taken place. They were already aware of their individual strengths and weaknesses and were able to share out tasks between them in a way that does not always happen in CMC conditions. I have seen CMC groups fail because no one is willing to lead, no one to reflect, and no one to do. I consider it necessary, if the group does not realize this for themselves, for the e-moderator to remind them of the need to set up groups, roles and processes through the online facilities.

These students quickly split this work between them and shared the strategic analysis process. Two of them logged in four times a day, but all six logged in at least once every day for all of the four weeks. Thus the group came to have a more synchronous feel. They were not online at the same time, but the flow of discussion felt continuous. My experience is that conference participants are better able to follow and contribute to one dominant thread rather than many. E-moderators need to sum-up and archive frequently, otherwise the ideas and arguments become tangled. Students may then look at the archive if they wish but focus on the topic under discussion. The advantage of CMC is that the texts of previous debates are still accessible and can be drawn on to enhance and develop the current discussion. Students may notice these linkages for themselves but the e-moderator can help make the connections.

I have to be abreast of the conference issues, and also have some knowledge of the material in the discussion. Only then can I be a summarizer, reflector and source of external support if group process fails, able to push along discussion if it becomes stilted, and to link discussion. My experience shows that these roles are important at the early stages of group forming rather than later. The group members become more capable of undertaking the roles for themselves once they are practised in the conference process. After the first two weeks I step back and allow them freedom to develop their ideas. If a member of the group is competent with the software, the e-moderator can also let the summarizing and archiving become the group's responsibility.

During week three of Case Study 2, the conference developed over 200 messages. I regularly archived the messages into online folders for ease of use. However, my interventions were light and I indicated if a particular approach was moving away from the case itself. As the participants saw more of value to them as individuals emerging out of the exercise, they became more committed to the process. I find this point in a conference most challenging to e-moderate. It is like a parent shaking a child free from the apron strings – a strange and uncomfortable feeling. Overactive e-moderating at this point will not enhance group working and may cause it to breakdown. This is the skill of e-moderating by silence!

When I asked the students why they thought these conferences were so successful, their answers were:

It was always worth logging-in.

It wasn't like popping into a conference to check if there is anything interesting, it was like catching up with your favourite TV show or magazine.

Not going into the conference was like coming off an addictive drug. I was at work wondering what new insights tonight would bring. I'd rush to the PC when I came in.

Although this level of interaction did not continue after the four-week case study was over, the group continued to work well together throughout the course and provided good support to each other for revision and examination preparation. They all achieved marks in the middle range for the final two assignments and had good passes in the examination.

On reflection, offering parts of the case over a fixed period was more effective than simply breaking the case into four areas of analysis (the Case 1 approach). By the end of four weeks of Case 1, students were fed up with it. For Case 2, the story kept moving on and a key strategic lesson was learnt, that the same tools and approaches were shown to work differently, even in the same organization, because of changes occurring in the internal and external environment of the organization. I therefore prefer this drip-feed approach, which is only possible through asynchronous online working, to an 'upfront' case analysis.

CMC systems

If you have already used CMC software, you may want to skip this section, in which I want to say just enough to introduce the software to those who have never seen it.

CMC provides a way of sending messages to a group of users, using computers for storage and mediation. A computer, somewhere, holds all the messages until a participant is ready to log on and access them, so online conferences do not require participants to be available at a particular time. For this reason CMC is often called 'asynchronous' (not operating at the same time), although synchronous (at the same time) 'chat sessions' use similar technology.

CMC serves people almost anywhere, because participants need only have access to a computer, a network connection and password, a modem and a telephone line to take part. You may have been in a cybercafé recently. They have appeared in many cities, world-wide. You can join a CMC network through any of them.

Three types of technology are involved in CMC:

1. **A server (special computer) and software system:** the server can be anywhere, though often it is maintained and housed by the institution or organization that sets up the CMC. It is a special computer, with its own software, that can store and organize well the CMC messages, of which there may be tens, even hundreds, of thousands in a year. Fast, powerful hardware and reliable, sophisticated CMC software enable many thousands of users to access CMC through a single server.

2. **A terminal or personal computer for each user:** there are two main ways of accessing the server. For the first, client access, an application program must be installed on each user's computer. Client software is produced by the same software company that designs and distributes the server software. It has powerful functions and features and is normally fast and reliable.

   Until recently, CMC was typically delivered through client software. However, it is now possible and common for CMC to be delivered through standard Web browsers and interfaces. Access to CMC through Web browsers needs no special installation and is catching on quickly since free browsers are now factory-installed on computers. This method of access at present provides fewer features and slower communication, and is not as 'slick' as client software.

3. **A telecommunications system to connect the computers to the server:** connections for the computers can be through local area networks that link the computers in a department, campus, region or country, or the computers can be connected through modem and telephone lines. Increasingly, networks are being linked, so that a message may cross several networks before it arrives in the relevant conference in the server. Students and trainees are able to access conferences through a home computer and telephone line, a work or campus computer (typically on a network) or a computer at a study centre or student residence.

CMC software

Some universities have developed their own CMC software and systems, but most educational and training providers choose a commercially available system because they want the benefits of support and development, year in, year out, at a reasonable cost. Lotus Notes, FirstClass and Web CT are examples of popular systems. There are many others. Each has its own underlying software 'engine', a different 'look and feel' for the participants, and different facilities and functions for e-moderators. Of course, all systems have certain features, but there are real differences.

For example, Lotus Notes provides a shared database system that is very powerful, therefore commonly used in industry. It offers good facilities where large groups are involved, with high security. However, the screen looks rather like a filing cabinet and there are few opportunities for e-moderators to choose graphics of any kind.

FirstClass, by contrast, provides a wide choice of icons for organizing conferences and discussion areas and is very popular in the United Kingdom. It can be accessed either through the Web or by 'client' software that is loaded on each user's machine. WebCT, developed in Canada, offers bulletin board systems for conferencing but also an easy-to-use authoring tool for developing online learning materials. There are some free Web-based systems that are easy to set up and try. (Follow the links in Resources for practitioners 21, Part 4: Software for CMC, at the end of this book, to find out more).

The examples throughout this book are drawn from e-moderating experiences using many different systems. It's probably true that if the e-moderators are keen and competent, having the best software system is rather less important as long as it doesn't crash!

CMC for education and training

Compared to face-to-face group teaching, for example, CMC is readily available, and does not require participants to travel to a certain place. Many users find that the time lags involved between logging on and taking part, encourages them to consider and think about the messages they are receiving before replying, rather more than they would in a class situation. Participants can ask questions without waiting in turn. Because of these characteristics, rather different relationships – usually based on shared interests or support – can develop compared to those between learners or teachers who meet face-to-face. Although many people find the lack of visual clues strange, messages are 'neutral' since you cannot see whether the sender is young or old nor need to consider their appearance or race. This characteristic of CMC tends to favour minorities of every kind and encourages everyone to 'be themselves'. Of course as CMC includes more pictures, as it certainly will, this situation will change again. Meanwhile with text-based conferencing it is possible to 'rewind' a conversation, to pick out threads and make very direct links. Therefore online discussions have a more permanent feel and are subject to reworking in a way more transient verbal conversation cannot be. This means that the CMC medium is good for giving praise and constructive critiques.

CMC can be viewed as a new context for learning, not just as a tool. It enables individuals and groups of people to carry on 'conversations' and 'discussion' over the computer networks. At present, CMC relies on the typed word, although audio and visual links are being added. CMC works like a series of notice boards, each with a title and purpose. For example, an individual may set up a conference and post a message on it to begin a conference. This message could be, 'This area is for our discussion on your next assignment'. Each participant then logs on through his or her personal computer, reads the message and can post one of his or her own. When the originator of the first message logs onto the conference a few days later, 20 others may have made their contribution to the discussion and perhaps responded to each other's questions. Participants continue to log on, read the contributions of others and the discussion proceeds. CMC's ability to engage its users is remarkable.

The asynchronous nature of CMC relates to many of its special characteristics. The benefits include the convenience of choice over when to participate. Participants can have 24-hour access to the system and can log on when they wish, for as long or short a time as they want or need to. Many participants can be logged on at the same time although each message appears in a list. CMC is less intrusive than face-to-face conversations or telephone tutorials because participants can choose when to read messages and when to contribute.

CMC involves a hybrid of familiar forms of communication. It has some of the elements of writing and its associated thinking, and some of the permanence of publishing, but it also resembles fleeting verbal discussion. The discursive style of the typical participant lies somewhere between the formality of the written word and the informality of the spoken. An experienced e-moderator wrote to one of his online students, 'Consider this medium as like talking with your fingers – a sort of half-way house between spoken conversation and written discourse' (Hawkridge, Morgan and Jelfs, 1997).

Being able to reflect on messages and on the topic under discussion, in between log on times, has always seemed important to researchers into CMC, and to some at least of the e-moderators I have known. It does seem that quite a few participants reflect on issues raised online and then mould their own ideas through composing replies. For example, a very experienced Open University teacher describes his first participation in an online conference:

> I was struck by how I'm still in touch with the conference even when away from my computer and busy with other activities. Somewhere in my unconscious I continue to debate and new lines of argument keep occurring to mind unbidden. And it is always so tempting to take just one more peep at the screen to see if another participant has come up with something new or built upon the last message one posted oneself.

(Rowntree, 1995: 209)

CMC can offer the opportunity for a whole series of ideas to be pulled together, too. Many computer conferences promote openness and, except in conferences that are deliberately and rigidly pre-structured, participants expect freedom to express their views and to share their experiences and thoughts.

The online environment for CMC mediates the communication but also shapes it. CMC enables large groups of people or selected sub-groups with common interests or purposes to communicate (Preece, 2000). Participants do not need permission to contribute and individuals can receive 'attention' from those willing and able to offer it. Face-to-face identities become less important and the usual discriminators such as race, age and gender are less apparent. Successful participation in CMC does not depend on previous computer literacy and it often appeals to inexperienced computer users.

Authority and control of the conferences may shift, at least temporarily, from teachers to students, trainer to trainee, the more frequently as the students become more competent and confident online. Existing hierarchies and relationships can change and even fade. The social and contextual cues that regulate and influence group behaviour are largely missing or can be invented during the life of the conference. It is easier to leave the conference unseen – and unembarrassed – than is possible in face-to-face contexts and synchronous chat sessions. It is also easy to 'lurk' or 'browse' – read conference messages but without contributing.

The lack of traditional hierarchies in CMC and its ability to support synthesis of knowledge lead to somewhat different styles of communication and knowledge sharing, compared to synchronous meetings. Programmes of study aiming at a spirit of wide access and openness, or at crossing industry, professional and international boundaries, are therefore well served, though such programmes are demanding in terms of technical access and learning support. The CMC environment is such that mistakes are rather public and recorded for all to see. Tardiness, rudeness or inconsistency in response to others tend to be forgiven less easily than in a more transient face-to-face setting. Minor complaints can escalate when several individuals in a conference agree with each other and create a visible 'marching about with banners' online.

For all these reasons, CMC has attracted the attention of leaders of graduate level courses, those involved in professional development of people such as managers and teachers, and those attempting to build online learning communities. Many have tried and some have been disappointed with their efforts to date: I hope they will find new insights and solutions in the experiences and approaches in this book.

CMC and costs

Anyone interested in introducing CMC into a course or teaching programme is likely to be asked the basic questions, 'What will it cost?' and 'Will it save money?' These are tough questions to answer, because every system is different, the technology is changing rapidly and opinions differ about how to estimate costs. Accountants, academics, administrators and politicians all have their own way of judging what is value for money. Accountants want to look at the 'bottom line'. Academics are conscious of the opportunity costs (such as time taken away from research or working with more familiar teaching systems). Administrators look for gains to the institution. Politicians want to foster national development.

As yet, there is no widely agreed method for working out CMC costs, despite concern about the costs of using online applications as additions to courses (Brown, 1998; Hawkridge, 1998). Nor is there a standard way to measure the educational or other benefits of using CMC (Bakia, 2000). In any case, what students and teachers actually do to learn changes when CMC is introduced, so meaningful comparisons are difficult. Within CMC, the costs and measured benefits of e-moderating alone have not been studied, since e-moderating is always associated with CMC systems, which in turn are based on courses or programmes. However, some studies are starting to show that by using CMC, higher student: faculty ratios can be achieved, with a satisfactory or perhaps increased learning experience. Innovation and collaboration costs money, too, for resources and time, and for the training and support of individuals (Bacsich and Ash, 1999). As Rumble (1999) says, costs of online learning depend so much on the context.

Average costs per student for CMC depend to some extent on scale but less so than expected due to the investment required in computer systems and the increased interaction between e-moderators and students (Mason, 1998). A virtual campus that saves on most of the capital and recurrent costs of buildings is not free, because at least some of the capital and direct costs of ICT infrastructures must be paid, but it may be cheaper (Tiffin and Rajasingham, 1997) or it may be possible to establish a 'crossover' point where the benefits of economies of scale come into play (Jewett, 1999; see also.www.calstate.educ/special-projects).

Some costs may be transferred or displaced. Hidden costs include the purchase of computing equipment and students' time. But savings may be gained through students using CMC instead of travelling to class (Bacsich and Ash, 1999). Rumble (1997) explores the accounting categories for online learning and gives an example of CMC costs on one large OU course in the early days.

Costing each activity related to CMC is difficult, but not impossible. Much depends on the assumptions behind the figures. For example, I compared the estimated costs of training Open University Business School e-moderators face-to-face with the actual costs of training them online. My estimates were based on costs in 1996 of a face-to-face weekend for 180 e-moderators, drawn from all over the United Kingdom and Western Europe, including travel and subsistence, attendance fees and set up costs, but excluding staffing costs and overheads. These came to £35,000 in 1996. The actual costs of the online training for 147 e-moderators totalled £8,984, again without including staffing costs and overheads. The two sets of figures do hide quite a few assumptions, but the cost advantage of using CMC was apparently considerable, in that particular context. For the Business School, there is a very substantial competitive advantage in having a large cohort of trained e-moderators, plus a proper induction programme for students, for all courses that use CMC, now and in the next few years. This advantage, if it could be costed, is probably worth far more than the total cost to date of CMC.

Rumble (1999) provides a comprehensive review of costs of networked learning including transfers of costs and qualitative cost benefits. Bacsich and Ash's approach suggests that networked learning costs should be based on all stakeholders – and that we will soon need to find a way of both planning for and recording the use of staff time (Bacsich and Ash, 1999).

Some commentators feel that the move towards incorporating the use of CMC in learning is in any case inevitable (at least for universities):

> The question is becoming, not whether flexible learning can enhance the cost effectiveness of traditional teaching (important though that question is), but whether a university will survive and prosper in the next century without rapidly integrating the various dimensions of flexible learning into its process, culture and value.
>
> (Moran, 1997: 181)

I hope this chapter has introduced CMC to you and started to explain the fascinating role e-moderators can play in enabling useful and productive online teaching and learning. Chapter 2 goes on to explore my research in this area.

To explore further the ideas in this chapter, look at the following Resources for practitioners:

1 Choosing a software system for CMC p101
3 Keeping e-moderating costs down p107
21 CMC Web sites p165

Chapter 2

A model for CMC in education and training

About the OU

My research into CMC for education and training was carried out in the Open University of the United Kingdom (OU), therefore you should know its context.

The OU is an excellent 'test bed' for new ways of teaching because it:

- is 'open as to people, places, methods and ideas' – and to new media;
- is one of the largest distance teaching universities with over 200,000 students world-wide;
- provides a wide range of supported self-study courses;
- awards its own internationally recognized degrees and other qualifications;
- is known for the quality of its teaching and research – and the success of its students.

Course design, production and distribution are located centrally at the OU's headquarters in Milton Keynes, England, together with personnel, finance and administrative systems. As the OU Website shows (http://www.open.ac.uk), on the Milton Keynes campus are the academic schools, faculties and institutes, as well as the administrative and operational departments and the BBC's OU Production Centre. I work in the OU's Business School at Milton Keynes.

Services to OU students, such as registration, advice and arrangements for residential schools and examinations, are devolved to 13 regional centres in cities of the United Kingdom. These are manned by administrative staff and faculty representatives with responsibilities for students and tutors. They look after some 300 study centres, in which the face-to-face tutorials take place, and they organize the residential schools, essential for students taking certain courses. They also recruit, appoint, induct, develop and supervise tutors, who are employed part-time by the OU as Associate Lecturers.

Tutors (mentors, instructors or teaching assistants as they are called in North America) have always had important roles in the OU system. Many people believe that the OU's success can be attributed to the support it gives to its students, through the tutors. Until the advent of ICT, each one tutored up to 25 students, mainly through the postal system but also through face-to-face group tutorials in the local study centres. They marked and commented on students' assignments, and students could phone them for support, direction and counselling.

For OU courses without CMC, this work has continued, but CMC has vastly changed some of these roles and functions for tutors, as I shall explain in this chapter. If you would like to know more about the development of CMC in the OU's courses, read Salmon (1999a).

Building a model of teaching and learning through CMC

Although e-mail was available to some OU students and tutors much earlier, CMC was first introduced in 1988, in a new course made by a team from the Social Science and Technology Faculties (*DT 200 Introduction to Information Technology*). As you can see from the title, CMC was peculiarly well suited to such a course. The course team, the tutors and the students were very keen to try it, if a little apprehensive about how successful it would be. The software available was CoSy; today, it looks very primitive, and it did cause some problems.

The DT200 course served about a thousand students a year for four years. The experiment was sufficiently successful for other course teams to want to include CMC as part of their media mix. By 2000, there were 160 courses, being studied by about 100,000 students, in which CMC was used. For the first time, one very large-scale foundation level course (*T171 You, Your Computer and The Net*) was taught entirely online. Many more courses with CMC were being made.

In 1991, the Open University Business School (OUBS) started experimenting with CMC in its Master of Business Administration (MBA) courses. During the early 1990s general interest conferences were provided covering topics of the students' choosing. They were available to those MBA students and tutors who wanted to use them and could – typically 20–30 per cent of students or 100–200 individuals per course. These first online discussions were seldom e-moderated except to start and stop conferences and to ensure that nothing obscene or inappropriate occurred (this was extremely rare).

I used these early voluntary conferences in the MBA to build simple working models of CMC use in the Business School. I developed a framework for action research, which allowed for pathways, ideas and feedback to be explored (Salmon, 1998a). My action research was aimed at solving problems rather than establishing theory. However, the models I created and developed provided a set of constructs that could be tested as well as a basis for later online induction and training programmes.

Methodology

My model as described below in some detail is therefore grounded in my research. Here is a very brief summary of my content analysis and focus group work, for those interested in exploring CMC action research.

First, I analyzed the content of messages. I concentrated on understanding the naturally occurring online behaviour. I was the observer. In CMC, every piece of information entered into the system, including all the messages, is stored and can be accessed. These messages are suitable units for content analysis (Holsti, 1968). There are many possible methodologies for studying communication patterns, but apart from content analysis they are too complex for non-specialists and not suitable for analyzing a huge volume of messages (Henri, 1992). CMC messages are in textual form but they have little in common with printed texts, the usual medium for content analysis, since they have been produced in collaborative and asynchronous ways. Each person's contribution has its own meaning and can be considered individually, although patterns of interaction and discourse can be ascertained. Messages in CMC have several advantages over printed texts when it comes to content analysis: the exactness of expression and the direct, brief and informative styles limited by software; the messages also form a distinct body, usually united by a joint purpose (Mason, 1993).

For my research, I printed around 3,000 messages over two years from the voluntary MBA CMC. I used 'idea units' for analysis (Potter and Wetherell, 1989). An idea unit is a single idea or piece of information, with its context attached. It forms a 'unit of meaning'. Like Halliday and Hasan (1989) I divided the idea units into univocal (received and understood) and dialogical (the text ceases to be a passive link in conveying information, and becomes a thinking provocation device).

Later, I did a content analysis of the responses to feedback from OUBS tutors undertaking online Tutor Training (described in Chapter 4). I created special conferences called 'reflections' where tutors could give feedback messages. I drew on Kelly's construct theory (Kelly 1955). I used a computer programme, COPE, based on cognitive mapping for data entry and analysis of the tutors' statements (Eden, Ackermann and Cropper, 1992). (COPE is now called Decision Explorer, see http://www.scolari.co.uk). COPE provided a powerful way of capturing the natural language used by the individuals in the conferences. I copied each statement from the reflections conferences in its entirety into the COPE software. I entered words and phrases exactly as the respondents gave them in their messages. COPE then acted as a database and enabled manipulation of the data to determine the most important ideas in a quantitative way, without loss of the original text.

After I had entered all the phrases and statements from the reflections conference, I searched for relevant text using the word search facilities and by listing concepts. The COPE database then provided a vehicle by which tentative classifications were made, changed, or extended. It provided basic retrieval and presentation commands and a variety of text-based and graphic displays and printouts of data (Eden, 1990). This enabled me to build a more complete picture of the statements. At any point in the analysis, I could ascertain the source of any statement. I colour-coded the statements according to whether they appeared to refer to technical aspects of the CMC software, learning aspects, or e-moderating and teaching. This analysis led me to revise the categorizations of some messages, and to a greater sense of the sequence of activities pursued by the online participants.

Second, I used focus groups, a rich source of qualitative data, to improve my understanding of participants' experiences (Morgan, 1988). I ran focus groups of 35 CMC participants who produced lists and mind maps. They employed brainstorming techniques and nominal group techniques (Van Grundy, 1988). I also asked them to draw causal maps of their experience of CMC. The focus groups provided a large amount of data in a short time, answering specific questions I had formulated from the content analysis.

From the lists and causal maps, I created process diagrams of what the participants considered were key activities for learners online, the significant technical skills needed, and the kind of support and help required. I built a simple model first, then obtained feedback and comment by showing the diagrams to further groups, to add to focus group results.

From 1996 onwards, with my OUBS colleagues I built and ran an e-moderators' training programme based on the first model. I was able to extend and test out the grounded ideas in the model. At the end of the first training programme in February 1997, accessed by 187 trainee e-moderators, I developed an extended model based on participants' experiences and opinions. I collected my data through online evaluation and reflection conferences during the training. Online training of a further 200 e-moderators in the OUBS during 1997–9 provided even more data, through 'reflection' conferences and exit questionnaires.

Five-step model

The consolidated model that I built from my action research is below. I hope you will explore it and use it in your own context wherever you can.

First let me summarize the model, before going into detail. Individual access and the ability of participants to use CMC are essential prerequisites for conference participation (stage one, at the base of the flight of steps). Stage two involves individual participants establishing their online identities and then finding others with whom to interact. At stage three, participants give information relevant to the course to each other. Up to and including stage three, a form of co-operation occurs, ie support for each person's goals. At stage four, course-related group discussions occur and the interaction becomes more collaborative. The communication depends on the establishment of common understandings. At stage five, participants look for more benefits from the system to help them achieve personal goals, explore how to integrate CMC into other forms of learning and reflect on the learning processes.

Each stage requires participants to master certain technical skills (shown in the bottom left of each step). Each stage calls for different e-moderating skills (shown on the right top of each step). The 'interactivity bar' running along the

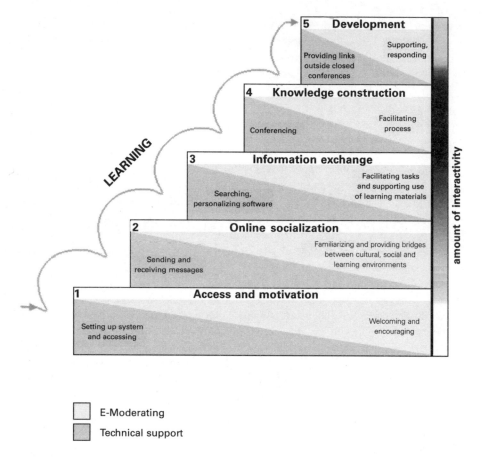

Figure 2.1   *Model of teaching and learning online through CMC*

right of the flight of steps suggests the intensity of interactivity that you can expect between the participants at each stage. At first, at stage one, they interact only with one or two others. After stage two, the numbers of others with whom they interact, and the frequency, gradually increases, although stage five often results in a return to more individual pursuits.

Given appropriate technical support, e-moderation and a purpose for taking part in CMC, nearly all participants will progress through these stages of use in CMC. There will, however, be very different responses to how much time they need at each stage before progressing. The model applies to all CMC software but if experienced participants are introduced to new-to-them CMC software, they will tend to linger for a while at stages one or two, but then move on quite rapidly up the steps again.

The chief benefit of using the model to design a course with CMC is that you know how participants are likely to exploit the system at each stage and you can avoid common pitfalls. The results should be higher participation rates and increased student satisfaction. E-moderators who understand the model and apply it should enjoy CMC and find that their work runs smoothly. This seems to be the experience of OUBS e-moderators, if I am to judge by the feedback from them. But let me go into more detail about the stages of the model.

Stage one: access and motivation

For e-moderators and students alike, being able to gain access quickly and easily to the CMC system is one key issue at stage one. The other is being motivated to spend time and effort.

If, like me, you are an organizer of CMC for education and training, you want to be sure that the student or trainee (I'll use the term 'the participant' for short):

- gets to know about the availability and benefits of the CMC system;
- sets up his or her own system of hardware and software;
- obtains a password, dials up or accesses the system through a network;
- arrives in the conferencing environment at the point where the conferences are available on the computer screen.

The participant needs information and technical support to get online, and strong motivation and encouragement to put in the necessary time and effort. Like learning any new piece of software, mastering the system seems fairly daunting to start with. Many participants need some form of individual technical help at this stage as well as general encouragement. Problems are often specific to a particular configuration of hardware, software and network access or else related to loss of a password. Access to technical support needs to be available, probably through a telephone helpline, particularly when the participant is struggling to get online on his or her own.

If you happen to be a participant who is paying for access to the Internet or for dial up calls, the amount of time spent online becomes an issue from the first log in. Time online is money. . . and if you make a mistake with CMC there is the added embarrassment of doing so in front of other people (not just the computer). No wonder some participants get nervous and need help!

Strong motivation is a prime factor at this stage, when participants have to tackle the technical problems. Stage one is when e-moderators can look out for any sign of life online from new students. This is the time to welcome participants and offer them support, by e-mail and/or telephone.

It is also motivating at the start to make very clear to participants the value of CMC, its links to and integration with the rest of the course, its role in assessed components (tests and assignments) and the amount of time they should allocate to its use. It is a great mistake to assume that any participant will want to divert hours and hours to online conferences without good reason. Clarity of purpose from conference designers and e-moderators is critical from the very beginning.

Stage one is over when participants have posted their first messages.

Stage two: online socialization

CMC offers the 'affordance' of online socializing and networking. Affordance means that the technology enables or creates the opportunity, ie it has an inherent social component. However, CMC will not in itself create the social interaction (Preece, 2000). Sensitive and appropriate conference design and the e-moderator's intervention cause the socializing to occur.

In stage two, participants get used to being in the new online environment. Many of the benefits of CMC in education and training flow from building an online community of people who feel they are working together at common tasks. However, such power is not inevitable but depends on the participants' early experiences with access to the system and integration into the virtual community. CMC has the ability to convey feelings and build relationships (Chenault, 1998).

A century ago, Émile Durkheim, the French sociologist, explored the issues and consequences of socialization and the implications of shared customs, beliefs and heritage for human behaviour and welfare. He is perhaps best known for his concept of 'collective representations', the social power of ideas stemming from their development through the interaction of many minds. He was of course writing long before anyone thought of the Internet but perhaps we could learn from the basic ideas as we start to build online societies? Durkheim showed that a sense of security and progress depends on broad agreement both on the ends to be pursued and on the accepted means for attaining them. Every grouping of people develops its own culture with formal and informal rules, norms of behaviour, ways of operating and sanctions against those who fail to understand or conform. An individual cannot easily replace a familiar culture or values with those of a new community – he or she is more likely to selectively adapt or modify features of a new group that seem attractive or useful. In this way a newcomer to an environment is assimilated but also changes the nature of the environment and the interpersonal interactions within it.

CMC is just such a new and potentially alien world for many participants. An influential discovery from the early research on CMC was the impact of the lack of non-verbal and visual clues in online interaction. Some participants regard this as an inadequacy that can result in a sense of depersonalization and hence negative feelings. Others consider the lack of face-to-face interaction to be a freedom and prefer that participants are undistracted by pictures of or the accents of participants, or by social games. Participants can disagree without arousing excessive emotion, they can debate without clashes apparently based on conflicting personalities and without shyer individuals having to 'fight their way in'. Some participants find it easier to ask for help online than face to face.

The virtues of a sense of time and place are those of finding 'roots' – provided by continuity, connectedness with place and others who share it and our own internalized set of instructions for how to behave, how to make judgements, feeling comfortable and 'at home in one's world' and the reassurance of the familiar.

When CMC fragments and expands this sense of time and place the usual pillars of well-being may be less available. There is evidence at stage two that individuals struggle to find their sense of time and place in the online environment. Hence the importance of enabling induction into CMC to take place with support and in an explicitly targeted way. When opportunities for induction into the online world are taken, participants report benefits to their later online learning.

In my experience, CMC participants display all these behaviours, needs and feelings, immediately following their gaining access to the system, when they reach stage two. They recognize the need to identify with each other, to develop a sense of direction online and they need some guide to judgement and behaviour. A wide range of responses occurs. Some are initially reluctant to commit themselves fully to public participation in conferencing, and should be encouraged to read and enjoy others' contributions to the conferences for a short while, before taking the plunge and posting their own messages. This behaviour is sometimes known as 'lurking', although the term can cause offence! 'Browsing' is perhaps a safer word. Some e-moderators become annoyed with lurkers but it appears to be a natural and normal part of CMC socialization and should therefore be encouraged for a while as a first step. It is also important that the e-moderators are tolerant of 'chat' conferences and online socializing. As Ari Leino, of the University of Turku said, following a CMC course across 22 countries, 'Chatting increases belongingness' (Leino, 1999).

When participants feel 'at home' with the online culture, and reasonably comfortable with the technology, they move on to contributing. E-moderators really do have to use their skills to ensure that participants develop a sense of community in the medium. Group discussions on the Web frequently demonstrate how quickly and easily group thinking and shared understanding can develop, often around the simplest of identity-bonding issues such as PC versus Mac, Canon versus Nikon. All of us who teach through groups know the tricks to get small face-to-face groups working quickly together – handing out a badge or a flag, allocating a space to sit, or working with a flip chart. We wouldn't dream of facilitating a learning or collaborating group without applying such basic principles!

The empathy developed through this stage of online interaction provides an essential prerequisite ingredient for later course and knowledge related discussions (Preece, 1999). At this stage e-moderators should take the lead in promoting mutual respect between participants, defusing problems and counselling any apparently alienated or offended individuals. They should also try to help those participants with similar interests and needs to find each other.

At this stage, it is essential to create an atmosphere where the participants feel respected and able to gain respect for their views. E-moderators should deal with strong differences of opinion or objections to procedures. The best way is in private through e-mail rather than allowing participants to 'flame' and cause discomfort in conferences. This is quite different from encouraging productive and constructive exchanges of views, which occurs at stage four.

This stage is over when participants start to share a little of themselves online. E-moderators should ensure that the social side of conferencing continues to be available for those who want it. Usually this is done by provision of a 'bar' or 'café' area and through special interest conferences. Skilled e-moderation will always be needed to ensure scalability of conferences beyond small groups. The balance between delegating the e-moderating responsibility and avoiding creating many, many small, unproductive conferences is a delicate one (Preece, 1999). E-moderating these can be time-consuming, and some large CMC programmes allocate e-moderators specifically for the social host role, perhaps recruited from experienced participants or alumni.

A trainee e-moderator reflected:

> For me, the key learning point from taking part in CMC is the realization that I am not alone in the problems I encounter. This is where this medium of communication scores over all others. Through reading the other messages you quickly find that whatever is concerning you, others have faced the same problem and that gives you confidence to carry on. CR

Stage three: information exchange

A key characteristic of CMC is that the system provides all participants with access to information in the same way. At stage three, they start to appreciate the broad range of information available online. Information exchanges flow very freely in messages since the 'cost' of responding to a request for information is quite low. In my experience, participants become excited, even joyful, about the immediate access and fast information exchange. They also show consternation at the volume of information suddenly becoming available. E-moderators can help them all to become independent, confident and enthusiastic about working online at this stage.

For participants, their learning requires two kinds of interaction: interaction with the course content and interaction with people, namely the e-moderator(s) and other participants. Whether on campus or in a distance learning programme such as OUBS's, content is usually best sent to participants as well-designed and carefully prepared print or by using videocassettes, CD-ROMs and other pre-recorded media. These days, content appears on Web sites too, mostly as text. Participants often find that references to course content, including links to online resources such as Web sites, provide welcome stimuli during CMC conferences.

E-moderators and participants alike soon find that the 'messiness' of conferencing is in stark contrast to well-crafted print or multimedia materials. CMC makes demands on the participants: they have to find what they really want. As two e-moderators in management education put it:

> It is very easy to see conferencing as a fun medium. This is possibly a valid use but my advice to participants would be to focus very clearly on what they want to get from conferencing and to pursue this objective as in any other management activity. RA

What a lot of files/conferences/folders – call them what you will. If I imagine a shelf of files for the various topics covered by our various conferences then it doesn't look too large and unwieldy but I must confess to a slight degree of cross-eyedness when scanning through all this. Having said the above, it is a super facility and great fun – as long as it stays manageable! CT

At this stage, e-moderators should ensure that conferencing concentrates on discovering or exploring known (to them) answers, or on aspects of problems or issues. Presenting and linking of data, analysis and ideas in interesting ways online will stimulate productive and constructive information sharing. E-moderating at this stage calls for preparation and planning, as in any good teaching.

Participants develop a variety of strategies to deal with the potential information overload at this stage. Some do not try to read all messages. Some remove themselves from conferences of little or no interest to them, and save or download others. Others try to read everything and spend considerable time happily online, responding where appropriate. Yet others try to read everything but rarely respond. These participants sometimes become irritated and frustrated. They may even disappear offline. E-moderators need to watch out for each of these strategies and offer appropriate support and direction to the participants. Information overload and time management is much less of a problem for those participants who are already well organized, or who rapidly learn to share the workload in teams.

At this stage, participants look to the e-moderators to provide direction through the mass of messages and encouragement to start using the most relevant content material. Demands for help can be considerable because the participants' seeking, searching and selection skills may still be low. There can be many queries about where to find one thing or another online. E-moderators should be introducing some discipline online through providing guidelines and protocols (see Part 2, Resources for practitioners). For participants, learning how to exchange information in conferences is essential before they move on to full-scale interaction in stage four.

The temptation at this stage may be to provide some kind of 'automatic' answering of frequently asked questions (usually called FAQs). See Masterton (1998) for an interesting researched example. It is common for overstretched e-moderators to insist that participants check electronic FAQs before asking online. This may work for technical issues or rules and regulations about the course if a good search programme is provided. However, it is unlikely to inspire appropriate communication around course content and best practice or lay the basis for more in depth interaction at stage four. At this stage, the motivation and enjoyment come from personal and experiential communication (Preece, 1999).

Stage four: knowledge construction

At this stage, participants begin to interact with each other in more exposed and participative ways. They formulate and write down their ideas or understanding of a topic. They read such messages from other participants and respond to them frequently and often successfully. As conferences unfold and expand, many (but not all) participants engage in some very active learning, especially through widening their own viewpoints and appreciating differing perspectives. Their grasp of concepts and theories is enhanced through the debate and by examples advanced by other participants. Once this process begins, it has its own momentum and power. Rowntree puts it this way:

> Participants are liable to learn as much from one another as from course material or from the interjections of a tutor. What they learn, of course, is not so much product (eg, information) as process – in particular the creative cognitive process of offering up ideas, having them criticised or expanded on, and getting the chance to reshape them (or abandon them) in the light of peer discussion. The learning becomes not merely active. . . but also *interactive*. The learners have someone available from whom they can get an individual response to their queries or new idea and from whom they can get a challenging alternative perspective. In return, they can contribute likewise to other colleagues' learning (and themselves learn in the process of doing so).
>
> (Rowntree, 1995: 207)

At best, highly productive collaborative learning may develop. As one OUBS e-moderator says:

> Conferencing is a medium that can add an extra dimension to developing ideas and increasing understanding of the course material. It gives the opportunity to stop and think and refine ideas without immediately losing one's place in a debate, and holds on to those ideas for future reference. It is important to accept that it has to be structured and focused in order to do that. IN

The issues that can be dealt with best by CMC participants at this stage are those that have no one right or obvious answers, or ones they need to make sense of, or a series of ideas or challenges. These issues are likely to be strategic, problem- or practice-based.

E-moderators have important roles to play at this stage. The best demonstrate online the highest levels of tutoring skills related to building and sustaining groups. Feenberg (1989) coined the term 'weaving' to describe the flow of discussion and how it can be pulled together. CMC makes weaving easier to promote even than in face-to-face groups, since everything that has been 'said' is available in the conference text. The best e-moderators undertake the 'weaving': they pull together the participants' contributions by, for example, collecting up statements and relating them to concepts and theories from the course. They enable development of ideas through discussion and collaboration. They summarize from time to time, span wide-ranging views and provide new topics when discussions go off track. They stimulate fresh strands of thought, introduce new themes and suggest alternative approaches. In doing all this work, their techniques for sharing good practice and for facilitating the processes become critical. While it is important to allow interest groups to flourish, it is also critical to allow them to die naturally away. The value of an online discussion can be very high while interest and focus last. There is no need to artificially extend these.

The locus of power in more formal learning relationships is very much with the tutor, teacher or academic expert. In CMC at stage four, however, there is much less of a hierarchy. You could say there is a 'flattening' of the communication structure between e-moderators and participants. E-moderating is not the same as facilitating a face-to-face group. In stage four, it may be necessary to explain this to the CMC participants, especially if they expect the e-moderator to provide 'the answers'. At stage four, we see participants start to become online authors rather than transmitters of information.

Particularly in distance learning, CMC has the potential for knowledge construction (not just information dissemination) at stage four (Murphy, 1999). Jonassen *et al.* assert that CMC enables this construction:

> Dyads and groups can work together to solve problems, argue about inter-pretations, negotiate meaning, or engage in other educational activities including coaching, modelling, and scaffolding of performance. While conferencing, the learner is electronically engaged in discussion and interaction with peers and experts in a process of social negotiation. Knowledge construction occurs when participants explore issues, take positions, discuss their positions in an argumentative format and reflect on and re-evaluate their positions.
>
> (Jonassen *et al.*, 1995: 16)

During my own research I undertook a study of groups of participants who had already reached stage four in their use of CMC. I examined three CMC conferences in an OUBS MBA course (*B820 Strategy*). The participants were charged with discussing the strategy of their chosen industry, with a view to deploying this new knowledge in their assignment. Extracts from these conferences can be found in Resources for practitioners 16 (p143).

In each of the three conferences different approaches developed. One group discussed the voluntary and not-for-profit industry. This sequence of messages started with a participant posing a series of questions. The e-moderator behaved like a participant and was unafraid to express a personal opinion. Message three, from a participant, suggested a structured way of capturing opinion – based on an audit. Several participants responded to this message and the audit reports became interwoven with a debate on stakeholders as customers. The participants were very aware of the need to be supportive and build on each other's contributions and of the communications protocols of conferencing in terms of length of messages, avoidance of mere lurking, and so on.

The second group discussed strategy in the brewing industry. This group had an interesting mix of participants, widely scattered geographically, who had never met. They appeared confident communicators and were operating in only information sharing and knowledge construction modes – there was no 'socializing' or technical discussion. The e-moderator was the managing director of a successful local brewery. Of the participants, around half were working in brewing and the rest were 'users', accustomed to drinking beer. The conference began with a participant drawing attention to a report on the brewing industry. He suggested that what he saw was the impact of the data and he asked for views. He also used a little self-disclosure about himself and his own job. Message two suggested that although the statistics were interesting, a wider view of the industry should be taken. Message three knitted together the first two messages and resulted in a very productive sequence of messages that attempted to weave understanding of quantitative ideas with notions of wider strategy. Many participants stated a view or gave information and then finished their messages with a question. Several messages from participants and e-moderators summarized and modelled ideas as well as supporting the contributions of others. The designated e-moderator had to do very little. About halfway through the sequence he too threw in a short message based on a question. The sequence closed after a participant commented on how useful the discussion was for the assignment.

The third conference was about strategy in the information technology industry. This conference also included a mix of participants, all managers working in the IT industry and customers. It had 30 active participants plus some lurkers. Although it had an e-moderator, this is an example of a conference where the participants effectively adopted and shared the e-moderating role, with one participant taking the lead. The participants spent considerable time and effort in defining their task and sharing ideas on how to collaborate. One participant adopted the e-moderating role by posting a starter suggestion and then continued to weave together other contributions. He then posted a plan which he later said '. . . has now been read by 31 members of the conference, ie a majority, without any objection'. He continued to facilitate the discussion throughout and his fellow participants much appreciated his role. This probably contributed later to their negative reactions to the official e-moderator's well-intentioned but directive interventions.

The conference continued by others posing questions, suggesting an online brainstorm and adding links to relevant Web sites. At the right moment, specific questions proved helpful in summarizing and focusing. While some participants interacted regularly, others came in only occasionally but nevertheless contributed effectively to the collaboration. Other participants acted as cheerleaders and timekeepers and reminded of the need for focus. They were extremely supportive and encouraging of each other's contributions which led to continuous development of the information sharing and knowledge construction. One participant managed a little humour – which is not easy online due to the lack of non-verbal expression. One 'lurker' apologized for his absence. There was good demonstration of search and share skills and of summarizing by participants.

The appointed e-moderator eventually felt he had to assert the requirements of the assignment in a very structured way, thereby establishing his authority rather than participating in the discussion. He thus gave the impression he was the teacher/assessor rather than adopting an e-moderating role. He asked for contributions from lurkers but this seemed to have no effect. He also asked participants to reduce the amount of 'techie' debate and for them to focus on the strategic issues. This resulted, some four days later, in one participant suggesting that they should join another conference. The e-moderator gained access for them and signed off with a 'good luck'. I conclude that the participants felt that the e-moderator was not helping them in the way they expected and that he was less skilled and understanding of online working than they were. Because of his inappropriate e-moderating approach, they sadly failed to succeed in tapping into any expert knowledge he had to offer.

All three of these e-moderators had been through the training programme using the model. Two had become very effective and successful e-moderators, one somewhat less successful. The latter continued to assert some authority, to the detriment of knowledge construction online, although he was known as a valued and effective face-to-face facilitator. I conclude that face-to-face facilitation skills, while having many of the same attributes as online e-moderation, are insufficient in themselves to ensure successful interactive conferences. Most participants have not 'grown-up' with CMC (indeed, some may still be mourning the passing of print), but this may change as the next generation enters professional and higher education. However, if some participants are also trained and experienced in conferencing skills, they may be able to take on successfully some at least of the e-moderating roles.

Stage five: development

At stage five, participants become responsible for their own learning through computer-mediated opportunities and need little support beyond that already available. Rather different skills come into play at this stage. These are those of critical thinking and the ability to challenge the 'givens'. At this stage, participants start to challenge the basis of the conferences or the system. They demand better access, faster responses or more software. They become extremely resistant to changes to or downtime on the system. It is also at this stage, however, that participants find ways of producing and dealing with humour and the more emotional aspects of writing and interacting. Experienced participants often become most helpful as guides to newcomers to the system. Indeed, a few who resent 'interference' wish to start conferences of their own and ask the designated e-moderators to withdraw. The participants are sometimes confident enough in the medium to confront an e-moderator when his or her interventions seem unhelpful or out of place. Some e-moderators are naturally concerned or upset about this since their roles are then difficult to negotiate.

At stage five, e-moderators and participants are essentially using a constructivist approach to learning. Constructivism calls for participants to explore their own thinking and knowledge building processes (Biggs, 1995). This personal knowledge includes not only ideas about the topic area under study, but also the teachers' and participants' responses to the experiences of teaching and learning themselves (Hendry, 1996). A key principle of constructivism is that the meanings or interpretations that people give to incoming information depend on their previous mental models and maps of the topic area or issue, drawn from experience.

When participants are learning through a new medium such as CMC, their understanding of the processes of using the software and of the experience of learning in new ways is being constructed too. It is therefore common at stage five for participants to reflect on and discuss how they are networking and to evaluate the technology and its impact on their learning processes. These higher level skills require the ability to reflect, articulate and evaluate one's own thinking. Participants' thoughts are articulated and put on view through CMC in a way that is rarely demonstrated through other media.

When conferences are set up to discuss the role of online conferencing in learning, they are always well populated with messages and ideas. The discussion probably includes uncertainties and problems with the content and design of conferences and an awareness of the social, ethical and technical dimensions of the experience of conferencing. E-moderators need to be prepared for this and should welcome it as evidence of real cognitive progress in their participants. E-moderators, for stage five, should set up exercises and online events that promote critical thinking in conference participants, such as commenting on each other's writing.

If suitable technical and e-moderating help is given to participants at each stage of the model, they are more likely to move up through the stages, to arrive comfortably and happily at stages three-five. These stages are the ones that are more productive and constructive for learning and teaching purposes.

Blumer's (1969) view of action learning is of people involved in directing their actions, individually and collectively, around shared understandings of their world. Each carry cultural, philosophical, physical and psychological luggage and shape their learning experiences to meet ends associated with these. The aspect of meeting online with colleagues, sharing views and receiving support, especially in terms of actions, is commented on time and time again in the conferences.

> I'm an enthusiast for getting in touch with someone (with more experience, or generous-spirited, or patient, or in an appropriate formal position, or stimulating to talk to. . .) and asking for help. All of you are here with me! RB
>
> I do like having the opportunity to computer conference. It breaks the isolation, it enables self-help, it networks, it allows for all kinds of learning styles. I wish I'd had this when I was studying my MBA. CB

There was evidence that the tutors going through the OUBS training were considerably altering their overall view of the world of CMC and their role within it. They seemed to be enjoying this experience: this is a first message from JD, a new e-moderator.

> I've never been in such an interesting new place. I'd just like to wish all conference members a happy New Year and to say how pleased I am to be starting this strange new programme. JD
>
> Thanks for the Christmas cheer giving me much food for thought, and so little thought for food! KH
>
> This experience has forced me to rethink, review and refocus! JB

An eclectic approach will not do the trick if you want to introduce CMC. If you want to encourage participants to move up through the stages, use online induction before a course starts (see Chapter 5). E-moderators also need online training beforehand (see Chapter 4). I am going to say more about e-moderators and their roles, with some examples, in Chapter 3.

The following Resources for practitioners will help you use the model:

5 Online participant induction p110
7 Using the five-stage model p115
9 Training e-moderators p123
11 Techniques for CMC Structures p127

Chapter 3

E-moderating qualities and roles

This chapter considers the knowledge and skills that the best e-moderators probably have, and uses examples to explore and illustrate their roles. I say 'probably' because what makes for good teaching has been the subject of many debates over the centuries, and a new debate is now going on in relation to online teaching. My intention in this chapter is to explore the qualities of e-moderation and to place the e-moderating roles firmly and significantly into the online learning environment. This chapter includes recruiting e-moderators and key aspects of their roles. It also offers you three examples of e-moderation in practice.

What do e-moderators do?

You already have some idea from Chapters 1 and 2 of what e-moderators commonly do. In the Open University, and many distance learning systems, the various aspects of teaching are divided up among several people. Usually, for example, the authors of course materials do not look after groups of students studying at a distance, whose progress is guided and evaluated by tutors. Authors are subject matter specialists and they may have training and experience in preparing print, audio and video materials. Tutors know something of the subject matter too but have training and experience in dealing with students. E-moderators could be described as specialist tutors: they deal with participants but in rather different ways because everyone is working online. An e-moderator, like a tutor, does the job part-time and probably has another job too: typically, this might be teaching, but it doesn't have to be.

Is CMC a unique communication medium? It lacks social and contextual cues and is not strictly controlled. It also generates new communication patterns. I have noticed that OU Business School course teams with CMC communicate much more directly and widely with tutors than those without. The tutoring community builds up online and tutors' exchanges are much more prolific and productive than when tutors meet only occasionally face-to-face. There is more sharing of experiences than is possible in face-to-face meetings. The style of writing online is an unusual combination of informal and formal. All these aspects are largely enjoyed and considered highly beneficial by the participants once they have become accustomed to using CMC. I think it is indeed a new context for learning and interacting, rather than simply mediating teaching. The conference users, both students and e-moderators, are creating and shaping the learning environment rather than having it imposed upon them.

As discussed in Chapter 2, each level of the five-stage model involves somewhat different activities for the participants. What the e-moderator does online, and how much, varies according to the purposes, intentions, plans and hopes for a conference – and of course with the motivation, knowledge and skills of the e-moderator.

CMC has often been adopted where programmes of study involve the sharing of professional or sectarian knowledge, such as management, teaching and technology. Interacting with peers and practitioners is especially important when the learning impacts on practice. CMC enables the sharing and assimilation of a wide range of experiences of practice. This form of knowledge is often informal, tacit and continuously developing. The participants create knowledge for themselves through dynamic processes as explained by levels three and four of the model. Therefore, in e-moderating there is very little teaching in the conventional sense of instruction or 'telling'. Online learning offers participants opportunities to explore information rather than asking them to accept what the teacher determines should be learnt. They construct knowledge for themselves through interacting online with peers, under the guidance of their e-moderator.

The e-moderator's main role is to engage the participants so that the knowledge they construct is usable in new and different situations. So you can see the goal of the e-moderator for this kind of learning is to enable 'meaning making' rather than content transmission.

E-moderator competencies

In Table 3.1 I have shown the qualities and characteristics of successful e-moderators – the competencies they should acquire through training and experience.

Table 3.1 E-moderator online competencies

Quality/Characteristic	1. Confident	2. Constructive	3. Developmental	4. Facilitating	5. Knowledge sharing	6. Creative
Understanding of online process	Confident in providing a focus for conferences, intervening, judging participants' interest, experimenting with different approaches, and being a role model	Able to build online trust & purpose; to know who should be online and what they should be doing	Ability to develop and enable others, act as catalyst, foster discussion, summarize, restate, challenge, monitor understanding and misunderstanding, take feedback	Know when to control groups, when to let go, how to bring in non-participants, know how to pace discussion and use time online.	Able to explore ideas, develop arguments, promote valuable threads, close off unproductive threads, choose when to archive, build a learning community	Able to use a range of CMC conferencing approaches from structured activities to free wheeling discussions, and to evaluate and judge success of conferences
Technical skills	Confident in operational understanding of software in use as a user; reasonable keyboard skills; good access	Able to appreciate the basic structures of CMC, and the WWW and Internet's potential for learning	Know how to use special features of software for e-moderators, eg controlling, archiving	Able to use special features of software to explore learners' use eg message history	Able to create links between CMC and other features of learning programmes	Able to use software facilities to create and manipulate conferences and to generate an online learning environment
Online communication skills	Confident in being courteous, polite, and respectful in online (written) communication	Able to write concise, energizing, personable online messages	Able to engage with people online (not the machine or the software)	Able to interact through e-mail and conferencing and achieve interaction between others	Able to value diversity with cultural sensitivity	Able to communicate comfortably without visual cues
Content expertise	Confident in having knowledge and experience to share, and willing and able to add own contributions	Able to encourage sound contributions from others	Able to trigger debates by posing intriguing questions	Carry authority by awarding marks fairly to students for their CMC participation and contributions	Know about valuable resources (eg on the WWW) and refer participants to them	Able to enliven conferences through use of multimedia and electronic resources
Personal characteristics	Confident in being determined and motivated as an e-moderator	Able to establish an online identity as e-moderator	Able to adapt to new teaching contexts, methods, audiences & roles	Show sensitivity to online relationships and communication	Show a positive attitude, commitment and enthusiasm for online learning	Know how to create a useful, relevant online learning community

Recruiting e-moderators

The e-moderators you recruit should of course be credible as members of the learning community. They do not, however, need a long string of qualifications, nor many years of experience. Nor do they need to be experts or gurus in the subject – as a rough rule of thumb, I suggest that they need a qualification at least at the same level and in the same topic as the course for which they are e-moderating.

I am going to assume that you will be looking for e-moderators able to understand their roles and willing to be trained online. They will need reasonably good keyboard skills, and some experience of using computers, including online networking. However, given those requirements, you will find that good e-moderators come from many different backgrounds, with very varied learning and teaching experiences. If they do not need to meet face-to-face with their course participants, you can select them on the basis of their suitability rather than their geographic location.

I suggest that you try to recruit e-moderators with the qualities from columns 1–2 of Table 3.1. At the moment, there are very few people available with these abilities. I tend to select applicants who show empathy and flexibility in working online, plus willingness to be trained as e-moderators. Before asking them to work online with CMC participants, train them in the competencies described in columns 3–4 in Table 3.1. I would expect e-moderators to be developing the skills in columns 5–6 by the time they had been working online with their participants for about one year.

Who might you work with?

Most e-moderator recruits come from face-to-face teaching where they may have relied quite heavily on personal charisma to stimulate and hold their students' interest. It is a big change to make when switching to CMC. Even those recruits who are used to developing distance learning materials need to explore how online materials can underpin and extend their teaching. If they are used to being considered an 'expert' in their subject, they may find the levelling effect and informality of conferencing very challenging to start with. It may be best to encourage such staff to undertake 'question and answer' or information exchange conferences until they become more comfortable with the characteristics of online discussion groups.

Conversely, students used to the paradigm of teacher as the instructor may expect a great deal of input from the e-moderator. This can be very time-consuming and unsatisfactory for both. The e-moderator must explain his or her role at the start, to reduce the chances of unreasonable expectations arising.

Key issues for e-moderators

A number of issues come up time and time again for e-moderating. Understanding these may make the difference between a happy and successful e-moderating experience and a miserable one. These issues include the appropriate numbers of participants in a conference, the use of time online, coming to grips with the asynchronicity and complexity of conference messages and the development of professional online communities. What follows is a brief exploration of these, which I hope will help those of you soon to encounter these in the real online situation.

What is the right number of participants in a computer conference for it to be successful? Is there a critical mass, in the physical sciences sense, so that with too few participants success eludes even the best e-moderator? The right kind of number for any conference depends fundamentally on its purpose. Six participants and an e-moderator, for example, may lead to all contributing and a collaborative outcome for an online activity. Or one thousand participants could pose questions to an online expert, and all read the answers. They might then join in smaller groups – perhaps of 20 each – to put their own views. Resources for practitioners 11 shows you that the right numbers depend on the purpose of the conference.

We know that starting off well with good welcoming messages helps very much. After that, part of the e-moderator's role is to try and orchestrate appropriate participation for the purpose. It is always necessary to try and keep track of what is happening to ensure participants do not disappear for reasons that can be changed! Most software systems offer features such as "message history" to help you track numbers and participation.

We have found that one of the best ways of building up the right numbers for a conference is to work with the energy that naturally builds up online (for whatever reason). You can certainly expect increased online activities to be associated with offline purposes, such as assessed assignments, the start of a new section on a course, periods just before face-to-face meetings or the run up to the exam. There may be unexpected reasons for increased online activity (eg a relevant news event or even a problem such as delayed arrival of course materials) and e-moderators can turn this to their advantage. When a conference or online activity naturally starts to wane, it is best to close it and start something fresh.

For trainee e-moderators, coming to grips with asynchronicity in CMC can prove very demanding because of the complexity of large conferences. The management tutors (see Chapter 2) certainly had some problems when they were being trained. Participants could 'post' contributions to one conference then immediately read messages from others, or vice versa. A participant might read all his or her unread messages in several conferences and then post several responses and perhaps some topics to start new themes. In any conference, this reading and posting of messages by a number of individuals can make the sequencing difficult to follow.

> One of the difficulties with this excellent FirstClass is that there are so
> many icons; it's like having a myriad of friends and not knowing who you've
> spoken to, who you've left a message with or who is expecting a reply. Any
> bright ideas – friends?
> Cheers, A :-) AB

This participant uses an emoticon to demonstrate that he is not being too serious
about this problem.

Since all the texts are available for any participant (or researcher) to view online,
the sequencing of messages, when viewed after a discussion is completed, looks
rather more ordered than during the build-up. Yet trying to understand them
afterwards is rather like following the moves of a chess or bridge game, after it is
over. When participants start using CMC, this apparent confusion causes a wide
range of responses. CMC can elicit quite uncomfortable, confused reactions from
participants and severe anxiety in a few. Although many people are now familiar
with e-mail they are not used to the complexity of CMC's many-to-many
conferencing, with its huge range of potential posting times and variety of response
and counter response. E-moderators can help, as one noted in his reflections:

> This is a very difficult but rewarding area. More effort is needed to keep
> even paced and also even-tempered at times. A conversation can be spread
> over several days without all the intervening gestures and interruptions of
> real conversation. This can lead to great misunderstanding. Thus to be
> reflective and not 'dash' off replies is important. To seek an even written
> style would hopefully bring some peace to bear, but the delay in reply which
> may be the result sometimes, of other commitments, can be annoying for
> colleagues. A welcoming and encouraging tone is vital, as being on the
> end of a computer, sometimes without a useful telephone conversation,
> can be very lonely.
>
> An e-moderator can ensure that all participants are familiar with the
> best the software has to offer and help them to be comfortable in the online
> environment to start with. A key e-moderating role is to build a clear
> structure by breaking conferences, if they get too busy, into sub-topics or
> sub-groups, and by regularly archiving and 'weaving' in summaries. PB

Nearly every participant, new or experienced, teacher or learner, worries about
how much time it takes to be online. You will find the concept of time is emotive
and value-laden for both e-moderators and participants. The key issue is that the
advantages of 'any time/any place' learning and teaching mean that time is not
bounded and contained as it is when attending a lecture or a face-to-face training
session. Although a face-to-face tutorial may last two hours, it has a clear start
and finish time and is rarely interrupted by anything else. The participants are
either there or they are not, and if they are, they cannot be doing much else.

CMC is not like that. It has a reputation for 'eating time'. Genuine fears and concerns do exist, and must be addressed.

It is important to specify the amount of time and what you expect e-moderators and participants to do and by when and not to leave this open-ended. It is of course important to design for the numbers involved in a conference, and be realistic about how much an e-moderator can do. Online novice learners and e-moderators will need much longer to do everything than experienced participants. Ensure that you use the most trained – and probably the most expensive – people (eg academics, faculty, experienced e-moderators) to do what they do best. Use less trained and experienced people, perhaps cheaper, for other tasks (eg use alumni as social hosts, or to run helplines shared with other schools). When choosing media and activities, make sure the time online is used for what it's good for rather than to force-fit activities into CMC. At the same time, reduce offline activities for participants by as much as you are providing online activities for them, so that looking after both sets does not overwhelm e-moderators. Be explicit about who is going to do what online, how much time you expect them to devote to it and what their payment rate will be. Ask them to do one or two important online activities in a time-bounded way, within a time limit, until they gain experience in managing their own online time. Develop and share a process of working together in e-moderating teams and in providing cover and breaks from online commitments. Develop and publish for all to see 'online office hours' and tell participants how much time e-moderators are being paid for so that there's a reasonable level of expectation about the frequency of online visits.

In CMC, as you know, there are three kinds of key players – the participants (students, learners, trainees), the academics (perhaps represented by resource material) and the e-moderators. Researchers, theorists and others can be brought in occasionally, too. It is exciting for participants to have access to expert views, though they may 'go quiet' and let the expert dominate, therefore it is best to keep such sessions down to a week or two. Craft knowledge can be passed on through anecdotes and stories without one individual 'holding the floor'. Some younger or less experienced participants may need to be explicitly drawn in and valued.

By learning through well e-moderated conferencing, each participant can construct his or her understanding according to previous experience and may make this explicit and available for others through the conference messages. The new information can be 'encoded' and learnt by other individuals through linking it to their previous knowledge. The emphasis that constructivism places on creating challenging learning environments, means that continued efforts need to go into training e-moderators and inducting students and to ensure that they understand the importance of online knowledge construction.

Success in using CMC seems to come where most networking occurs and where there is openness and freedom to explore with little risk attached. In the OU's Business School, for example, CMC is more successful in the open MBA courses, which have students from many backgrounds, than in closed company environments. This is true even though the corporate sponsors may provide hardware, software and financial support for their staff taking the MBA. Henley

Management School also report CMC's success, with students using Lotus Notes, in their *Inter*-company MBA (Robinson *et al.*, 1998).

With our present state of understanding how to develop and disseminate knowledge online, e-moderators need credibility in the field of study. When professional knowledge is shared in face-to-face meetings, it has been easy to recognize others as 'one of us'. The e-moderator should therefore establish his or her credentials as a like-minded and experienced professional – and probably needs to work a little harder at this online than in a face-to-face group. E-moderators will also need to develop good working relationships with librarians – who are themselves rapidly transforming themselves into ICT resource providers.

Teacher education offers an example of building online learning communities with an impact on professional practice, going well beyond what is possible in specific training events (Selinger and Pearson, 1999; Leach and Moon, 1999). By working in such a community, participants can extend their networking beyond the institution in which they work. They can also work with others from different educational traditions. Selinger shows us that this aids their attempt to seek out and understand new ideas and opinions. Teacher trainees explore new ways of tackling everyday problems and report the results to the online community. The e-moderator's role in such a rich and professional environment is both rewarding and demanding (Selinger and Pearson, 1999).

In a global and technological corporate environment, large-scale electronic networking is proving very beneficial. Shell Technology Exploration and Production is undertaking a major move towards learner and business-centred employee development. Shell has created three core Internet networks, which reflect key areas of the business. Some 2,500 employees log in and take part every week. The conferencing is carefully structured and e-moderated (Loknes, 2000).

E-moderating with synchronous CMC

In the United States, and in some other parts of the world, distance learning often means learning in a location many miles away from the classroom where the teacher is. Many universities and colleges have installed video conferencing equipment that enables them to deliver the teaching to the distant locations. This is synchronous classroom teaching, but has little to do with asynchronous CMC.

However, synchronous CMC can be set up on the Internet. The most basic kind is the text-based chat session that anyone can join. The software shows each participant who else is online at that time, and messages can be addressed to one, some or all of those 'present'. These messages appear almost instantaneously on the screens of all participants, inviting immediate responses. Beyond the mere text, users with the right hardware and software can add sound and vision, though these add complexity too because everyone can't speak at once. The learning environment becomes more like that of a telephone conference call, or even a videoconferencing session.

These technologies allow for real-time communication: users are online together at the same time and speaking or writing to one another immediately.

Synchronous 'events' need planning and an e-moderator may be badly needed to avert chaos. They can add a sense of presence and immediacy that is attractive to participants, some of whom find they can engage and get to know others. Many find that being online together is fun, so long as the experience is short, say half an hour or less.

Synchronous applications of ICT are sometimes combined with other media for educational purposes in order to get the motivating impact of e-event but with the potential for some deeper learning. For example, a Webcast, which is like a TV broadcast but delivered through the Internet, can be combined with incoming synchronous messages from all 'viewers' of the broadcast. This enables the presenter to immediately pick up and respond to questions and comments (Pullen, 1998; Scott and Eisenstadt, 1998).

The role of the e-moderator in online synchronous discussion reflects some of the qualities of the asynchronous e-moderator, especially to focus the conference at the beginning, keep it roughly on track and summarize it. Achieving full participation by the students through ensuring everyone 'takes a turn' is also an important e-moderating role. The software may offer special rights to the e-moderator, who can use the technology to control turn taking.

If you are involved in this kind of e-moderating, the usual 'rules' apply. You need to be familiar and comfortable with the applications and aware of their strengths and weaknesses as learning tools. Participants soon spot a teacher who is unfamiliar with the equipment. As always, good preparation for the event is essential. You need to allow time to get ready for the online session and for follow up. Critical success factors are good clear structure to the session, the quality of the visual materials, the clarity of the objectives and roles of the participants and ensuring everyone participates. If your participants can see you, you may need to brush up on your presentation skills! You should also plan to follow up the synchronous online event with a record or action plan, perhaps using e-mail, asynchronous conferencing or post.

Qantas College Online case study

Tony Fiddes is Manager of Qantas College Development. He describes how he set up online training in Qantas Airlines, a large corporation with offices and plant worldwide. He describes the creation of e-moderators from a group of skilled and experienced face-to-face trainers.

> Our experience with Qantas College Online to date has shown that creating successful online learning includes course design, administrative and management support, but the role of the online e-moderator is critical.
>
> Qantas College Online (QCO) was established in 1996 to provide greater access to training for all staff within Qantas Airways. QCO

uses the Internet to deliver a broad range of corporate development and training programs. Qantas chose the Internet as the delivery platform for the Online College as it enables staff to access training from anywhere around the world at anytime. Through QCO staff have access to:

- course, competency and qualifications information;
- course enrolment;
- interactive online course materials;
- support from tutors;
- e-mail, asynchronous noticeboards, synchronous chat;
- library services.

Participants can enrol and start at any time that suits them and their business units, although we are experimenting with group starts to help with interaction. The courses are designed to be learner-paced but they contain assessment tasks that require feedback from a tutor.

Asynchronous discussion conferences (noticeboards) are built into each course to encourage reflection and interaction. Tutorials are available through synchronous online chat facilities.

The role of the tutors as e-moderators is now becoming clearer and performance indicators have been established. These are all discharged through the online environment. QCO expects e-moderators to carry out the following duties:

- welcome and encourage participants to progress through the course by:
- send a welcoming e-mail within 48 hours of participant enrolment;
- monitor the progress of participants online to ensure that they are making reasonable progress through the course;
- provide online feedback on progress to participants;
- provide feedback to learners on learning activities in a timely manner by acknowledging receipt of participants' work within 48 hours;
- provide appropriate feedback on participants' submitted work within 7 days;
- convene and facilitate online tutorial sessions at times agreed with Qantas College;
- moderate noticeboards discussions by monitoring active noticeboard discussions at least once a week;
- provide input to noticeboards as appropriate;
- assess participants against learning outcomes by ensuring that the participant has met all assessment criteria associated with the learning outcomes;
- maintain participant records by keeping notes of participant interactions using tools provided in QCO to track learner participation, identify those learners who need further assistance and maintain assessment records;
- update status of participants using tools provided in QCO.

Abacus Virtual College case study

Gerry Prendergast is Training Director of Abacus Virtual College, which provides large-scale online training courses in the United Kingdom using FirstClass. He gives an example of using CMC for his Online Tutorial Asynchronous Workshop, an attempt to capture the reflection associated with asynchronous learning plus the motivation and commitment more easily achieved with synchronous activities. Gerry shows us the importance of careful but flexible planning. You will note the e-moderator's sensitivity to feelings and how this awareness relates to the rates of participation. Gerry's role as the e-moderator (and reflector) is explained as the process unfolds.

Course participants cannot always attend our scheduled face-to-face sessions. Recently, I discovered that none of my group could travel to a central location in order to attend their course final face-to-face day. I decided to try to achieve an 'end of process' event using FirstClass. Its time delays give participants a greater chance to give reflective responses and help to reduce the connection time and costs. I canvassed the participants to ensure that everyone could participate, at least for part of the session. I planned the event prior to the day, just as I would for a face-to-face learning session. A few days prior to the event, I posted the schedule online.

On the day, the activity started a little slowly, with participants first logging in, between 8.36 am and 10.10 am. I started with the following activity, at 8.51 am:

> Hi All,
>
> Welcome to the online module 5!
> The first area I want to look at is your original hopes explored as this course started!
> What I would ask each of you to do is to:
>
> Think about what your original hopes were
>
> Then
>
> Contribute: Which of them were realized/not realized and your feelings about these now?
> Post your message
> Log back in 5 minutes later and comment on anything that someone else has said.
> Gerry P

Initially, the participants spent some time acknowledging their presence on the system and socializing with their colleagues ('Good to see you online', 'What is the weather like in?'). I had not planned for the socializing but I realized it was important. This took almost an hour. The first of the answers to my question (shown above) was posted at 9.43 am. The next contribution was posted at 9.49 am. A number of other contributions then followed.

At 9.48 am I posted a second activity (a review of the participants' fears as stated at the start of the course). We now had two separate items under discussion running at once. This is very difficult to undertake in a face-to-face session but worked online. During the day, I found that I was able effectively to run up to three different discussions simultaneously.

The pace of participants posting contributions quickened considerably, as the morning went on. I decided to introduce short breaks, as contributors reported online fatigue. Some participants used this 'down' time to catch up and post more contributions. As the e-moderator, I used the time to review the progress made and to consider what I could hope to achieve after we resumed.

The participants started to log in again during the early afternoon and we again had an intense period of asynchronous discussion. By 3.15 pm I was feeling extremely tired and I became aware that others felt the same. I posted the following message:

> Has anyone else noticed how our style has become a lot more relaxed since we came online early this morning? I think it has a lot to do with us getting tired – it really takes it out of you communicating with five others online all morning.

Among the responses was the following:

> Me too, I thought we were logging in at set times, I have to admit my eyes are struggling as is my brain!

At this stage, the average number of contributions posted by each participant was just over 46. Many of these were two or three line responses, but a substantial number were over 10 lines long and contributed some excellent learning points to the group. At 3.31 pm I called a halt to the proceedings and ensured that a summarizer was appointed.

The results were extremely successful as everyone had fully participated, enjoyed and benefited from the experience and focused on the tasks. The event generated great camaraderie and teamwork and even some online humour.

Open University Centre for Modern Languages case study

Marie-Noëlle Lamy, Lecturer in French at the OU's Centre for Modern Languages, gives us a fascinating insight into two contrasting e-moderating techniques. By the way, Marie-Noëlle warns us that the French versions of the messages are unedited, and therefore contain mistakes.

> In language learning, chatting can be a legitimate learning outcome. If the 'chat' is not only in the language but also about language, the benefits of the interaction are heightened. Facilitating language aware-ness online thus offers the e-moderator a chance to let social needs work in favour of subject knowledge rather than as a distraction.
>
> Open University students of French as a Foreign Language used a bulletin board to take part in 'conversations' about vocabulary learning. The e-moderators used strategies involving different degrees of online visibility. Some were at times highly interventionist, pushing students to develop their subject knowledge, be more reflective, and find ways around their problems of learning in isolation without access to sources of expertise or information. To achieve these aims, however, they relied to some extent on traditional teacher-centred techniques, such as directing, instructing and asking questions to which they already knew the answer, in an explicitly tutorial way. For example, a learner sets off the enquiry and, in the absence of a dictionary or other information, states an erroneous hypothesis:

> Je n'ai aucune d'idée ce qui veut dire 'dicible'. Peut-être la phrase 'au-delà du dicible' veut dire 'the back of beyond'?
>   Amitiés

The English translation is:

> I have no idea what 'dicible' means. Maybe the phrase 'au-delà du dicible' means 'the back of beyond'?
>
>   Greetings

There is solidarity but no help from a second learner, indeed, he confirms the error!

> Il y a toute une gamme des choses d'intérêt pour moi parmi votre coup d'essai. Je n'ai trouvé pas 'dicible', mais j'aime la traduction 'the back of beyond'.
>   A bientôt

The English translation is:

> There is a range of interesting things as far as I'm concerned in your 'first attempt'. I couldn't find 'dicible', but I like the translation 'the back of beyond'.
>   See you soon

Here is the e-moderator's response to both learners:

> Pensées sur le travail de C-met d'E-h
> Merci, vous deux, car avec de courts messages, vous avez posé des questions importantes. D'abord, prenons le problème des informations qui ne sont pas dans le dictionnaire. Dicible n'y est pas. Mais réfléchissons: nous avons tous dans la tête des connaissances qui peuvent nous servir. Par exemple: dicible est de la famille de dictée, diction, et même bénédicité. Quel est le sens qui est en commun à tous ces mots? Pouvons-nous par conséquent déduire le sens de: au-delà du dicible? QUI VA REPONDRE?

The English translation is:

> Thoughts on the work of C-m and E-h
> Thank you to both of you, because, in your short messages, you have asked important questions. First, let's take the problem of when the dictionary just doesn't have the information you're looking for. 'Dicible' isn't in there. But let's think: we all have at the back of our minds some knowledge which can help us. For example 'dicible' (expressible) is related to 'dictée' (dictation), diction (diction) and even bénédicité (benediction, blessing). What is the meaning that all these words have in common? WHO WILL ANSWER?

The two students were able to respond to this prodding, and their messages, posted on the same day, showed how they had both surmounted the original difficulty. First came a new idea from the original enquirer (this time a good interpretation of the French).

> Bien entendu! 'dic' veut dire 'speak' (du latin, si je m'en souviens), mais 'speakable'??!! Donc, je pense que peut-etre la phrase 'elle aimait la solitude au-delà du dicible' veut dir 'she loved solitude more than words can say'. Est-ce que j'ai raison?

Or, in English:

> Of course! 'dic' means 'speak' (from Latin if I remember right), but 'speakable'??!! So I think that maybe the phrase 'elle aimait la solitude au-delà du dicible' means 'she loved solitude more than words can say'. Am I right?

A further contribution from the second learner:

> Moi aussi C-M! Je suis d'accord.
> (Enfin, un éclair de génie ('flash of inspiration', je l'ai trouvé dans le CD).J'ai cherché les exemples de la famille dic, et en commun est le sens de 'parler' ou 'parler à quelqu'un'. Bien, 'au delà du dicible' devient 'beyond saying, or more than could be said', afin de dire que Barbara vécût la campagne parce qu'elle aimait la solitude plus qu'on va dire.

In English:

> Me too, C-M! I agree.
>   At last, a flash of inspiration (I found that phrase in the CD).I looked for examples of the DIC word family, and in common they have the meaning of 'speak' or 'talk to someone'. OK, so then 'au delà du dicible' becomes 'beyond saying, or more than could be said', to mean that Barbara lived in the countryside because she loved being alone more than we will be able to say.

In total, this exchange was a success in that students identified a problem that interested them and used their existing knowledge of language by way of a generalized strategy for coping with lack of information. They arrived at a solution which satisfied them. However, it remained close to a traditional teacher–learner dialogue, and students were not inspired by it to contribute wider, more naturalistic language.

In contrast, other e-moderators preferred to intervene as little as possible, and to let students become 'teachers' for their peers. Here, a student requested help with the meaning of *obligation dramaturgique*, a phrase which she had found in a newspaper article, but which she was unable to discover in any dictionary. The first person to come to her aid (D) alerted her to the importance of 'context' and offered two possible solutions:

> Je suggère que cette phrase veut dire 'le besoin d'être vu de faire quelque chose ou le besoin de faire un récit mimé d'un rôle' mais on désirerait d'avoir plus d'information en ce qui concerne le contexte de cette phrase. Est-ce que ma suggestion saisit la signification de votre phrase dans son contexte? D.

In English:

> I suggest that that phrase (obligation dramaturgique) means 'the need to be seen doing something, or the need to tell a story in mime,' but it would be good to have more information about the context of that phrase. Does my suggestion capture the meaning of your phrase in its context? D.

After a clarification by the original enquirer, a second student, MK, offered a different approach: he used an analogy derived from personal experience to illustrate the phrase and offered a translation.

> J'aime bien la vie publique et il y a vingt-sept ans que j'étais fonctionnaire pour un conseil régional. La phrase 'une obligation dramaturgique', dans le context que tu as expliqué, fait comprendre à moi la phrase, 'a ritual dance'. C'est une phrase que tous les fonctionnaires utilisent entre eux-mêmes quand les conseillers discutent et jouent des roles adversariales comme dans une pièce de théâtre. Ils montrent les émotions artificiels, ils simulent être en colère quand en réalité c'est simplement la système de débat contradictoire. Pour le grand public c'est excitant, pour les fonctionnaires c'est très très ennuyant. MK.

Here is the English translation:

> I enjoy getting involved in public life and twenty-seven years ago I worked on a local council. In the context which you gave, the phrase 'obligation dramaturgique' suggested to me the phrase 'a ritual dance'. It's an expression which council officers all use amongst themselves to refer to the way councillors discuss things, taking up adversarial roles, as in a theatre play. They display artificial emotion and simulate anger when actually all that's going on is the normal course of a contradictory debate. For the public at large it's exciting, for council officers it's very very boring. MK.

E-moderator 'invisibility' certainly has its place in language learning online, at specific stages of the communication. These students learned something from each other about an item of French vocabulary. However, unlike the pair who discussed 'dicible' with their teacher, these ones did not gain access to generalizable learning skills. The challenge is to marry the two approaches, and devise an e-moderating style which moves learners in and out of two contrasting learning situations: one in which there are precise instructions for production of the outcome, and one in which productions are part of the socio-cognitive life of the online group.

Celebrate!

We need to mobilize and deploy the brains and commitment of teachers and trainers of all kinds in the service of e-moderating. We also need to raise the profile of e-moderators, and recognize and reward their valuable work. E-moderating is somewhat less visible (sometimes almost invisible if done well) and therefore special efforts need to go into celebrating good practice! I hope the exploration of roles and qualities in this chapter is of use to you and will enable you to recruit and train for very productive online teaching and learning.

To turn the ideas from this chapter into practice look at the following Resources for practitioners:

7 Using the five-stage model p115
11 Techniques for CMC structures p127
15 Knowledge sharing and construction p141
18 Communicating online p157
19 Valuing online diversity p161
22 What will we call ourselves? p169

Chapter 4

Training e-moderators

This chapter is about the process of creating e-moderators through training online in all their roles. I shall use as my main example the online training programme developed in the OU Business School.

Plan to train

Any significant initiative aimed at changing teaching methods or the introduction of technology into teaching and learning should include effective e-moderator support and training, otherwise its outcomes are likely to be meagre and unsuccessful. Even where technological infrastructure and support are strong, and when worthwhile learning applications are developed, without staff development nothing is likely to happen beyond pilot schemes. In the medium term, the costs of training and support for users can be higher than the provision of the technology; therefore it is worthwhile giving the training of e-moderators due consideration and adequate planning.

If you are feeling enthusiastic about developing CMC for learning, please be aware that a fair bit of rethinking of course methodologies, and of training and support for e-moderators, is needed for success. There are examples where, despite early adoption of CMC, courses reverted to old technologies. This is often due to the lack of support and development of teaching staff, or failure to manage the necessary organizational changes appropriately, or an inability to train sufficient e-moderators for expansion and development. E-moderating is not a set of skills any of us is born with, nor one that we have learnt vicariously through observing teachers while we ourselves were learning. As yet there are few online mentors to guide us through step by step. Maybe in the future, adults will draw on their childhood online experiences and try to emulate the examples of good e-moderators who changed the direction of their lives! But, meanwhile, e-moderators must be trained.

Because the pace of change is fast, few of us can allow for long apprenticeship through learning, supporting and then teaching in the online environment. It is likely that pressures will build up – either because student numbers are large or you want to be sure of early success – and gradual change may prove too slow. Critically, you must know what you are training for, and, as in any planning of learning activities, what competencies or outcomes you are seeking. Figure 2.1 in Chapter 2 gives you a suggested list on which you can build, bearing in mind your discipline, your students and your context.

Training must take into account the contentious issue of how much time e-moderators can be expected to work online. The time required depends on what they are doing, of course, but you can be absolutely certain that if they are untrained they will take longer and do it less well. As I have said, teaching online needs careful planning and preparation, otherwise the stories will continue of e-moderators being overloaded, underpaid and burnt out by the work.

Training of e-moderators in the OUBS

This chapter offers an example of large-scale training in e-moderating. I describe the steps that I took, with my colleague Ken Giles, in developing and implementing an online training programme for e-moderators in the Open University Business School, 1996–99. Each stage in the model that I explained in Chapter 2 provided a 'scaffold' or guide for training up e-moderators from novice to expert status in and through CMC. I hope that this account of our experience will be of value to you if you are facing similar training requirements whether on a small or large scale, in whatever discipline.

When we built the first online CMC training programme during the winter of 1995–6 in the OUBS we were faced with a fairly major task. Human and financial resources were limited. We wanted to use the five-stage model for CMC described in Chapter 2 as a basis. We expected up to 200 trainees, spread over most of Western Europe – it turned out that 187 registered for the first round of training. They were appointed to work as part-time tutors for the OUBS from home and most had full-time management or academic jobs outside the OU. We could assume that they had basic computer literacy although a few had more advanced skills. E-moderating through CMC was but one aspect among many of the teaching strategy and of their role as tutors for the MBA courses. CMC had to be meaningful and worthwhile for both the students and their e-moderators if it was to be judged a success.

We wanted to indicate to our trainees that CMC was essentially a distance medium of communication and to demonstrate that the training objectives could be achieved at a distance. We therefore considered that the training programme should use CMC itself and be accessed from tutors' own machines, probably at home. The tutors' first need was to be able to log in using their particular configuration of hardware from their home base, rather than using someone else's configuration via a different access point. The tutors truly needed to experience, much as their own students would, the pitfalls and the potential of CMC if they were to e-moderate effectively. A further very real reason for using CMC for the training was that to offer intensive face-to-face training would have stretched our human resources and provision of training facilities to the limit. Furthermore we wanted the training to focus on pedagogical knowledge, built up through personal and collective reflection on practice, rather than on acquiring a technical grasp of the hardware and software.

We were reluctant to ground the training in any form of text-based instructional materials, although this is common throughout the OU, because of the risk of these materials being divorced from the construction of the online knowledge and skills. However, it rapidly became obvious that a booklet, showing exactly what the screen should look like at each point in the procedure, was essential and we produced one for the second and subsequent versions of the training. To prepare the booklet, we had to create the online programme first, then print exact copies of the screens and key messages. This booklet supports those who like a paper manual. It also enables them to work offline if they wish, and they don't need to print pages for themselves.

Our training programme had to accommodate people with a wide range of prior skills and knowledge. The programme needed to be intrinsically motivating and lead to competent practice. The task was therefore to develop a programme that, while providing the development of essential basic skills (such as confidence and competence in using the software), represented as closely as possible the realities of teaching and learning online.

We decided the following:

- An average tutor would be expected to devote some ten hours to the CMC training programme.
- The design would be based on the five-stage model previously developed.
- A core of online e-moderators (online trainers of the online trainers) would be selected and trained to e-moderate the individual training conferences within the programme.
- Evaluation and action research would be based on tracking the trainees through the stages in the programme by a series of online conferences and questionnaires of a quantitative and qualitative nature and through monitoring the work of the trainees online after the training finished and the tutors commenced working with students.
- A small fee and a sum for telephone expenses, and a certificate of completion, would be provided that the trainees could claim on completion of their exit questionnaires.

Training programme design

We planned for a wide range of prior knowledge and/or experience of CMC among the trainees. Each would have his or her own 'map' of the topic. The programme needed to include training in declarative knowledge – what is this icon?, procedural knowledge – how do I send a message? as well as more strategic knowledge – what can I do with my e-moderating skills? However, we planned that trainees would acquire these various kinds of knowledge in an integrated way. The online training programme would not only be about acquiring new skills but would also help trainees to explore their attitudes to CMC and its meaning for their own teaching.

We took a number of decisions at this stage about our own approach to online training. The programme was designed to create a series of 'microworlds' in which the trainees could interact with each other, with the e-moderators of the training conference (who we called convenors) and with the software, before progressing to the next stage. We hoped that our trainees would gradually build up their knowledge and software skills, particularly in the use of computer conferencing for management learning. We made them aware of the goals all the way through the training. They were advised of appropriate ways of undertaking the tasks but could also construct their own approach. We tried to enable them to use the software as a matter of routine while we raised their awareness of the teaching and learning aspects. The importance ascribed in constructivism to the building of relationships between new and existing knowledge (Bruner, 1986) led us to a careful choice of icons and titles for conferences, and the use of familiar metaphors for explaining aspects of CMC.

Helping trainees to control their frustration is a key aspect of learning to use CMC. We tried to achieve a balance between a trainee struggling with too much complexity and being given enough involvement in the task. We attempted to give more help when trainees got into difficulties and less as they gained proficiency. In practice some trainees needed almost no help and others huge amounts. It did not prove possible to predict who needed extra help until they asked for it. So it was important to provide a continuously available source of help.

Evaluation

Engaging in reflective and interactive online activities, especially those leading to explaining, justifying and evaluating problem solutions, is a very important learning process. In 1983, Schön pointed out that people change their everyday practice by having reflective conversations, they frame their understanding of a situation in the light of experience, and they try out actions and then reinterpret or reframe the situation in the light of the consequences of that action. Schön also argued that through reflection a practitioner could surface and critique understandings that have grown up around a specialized practice and make sense of a situation for him or herself. We think this applies to online training too.

We wished to find ways of enabling reflection on CMC practice to happen within the training programme, at each of the five levels. We therefore decided to introduce a set of simple motivational goals, by requiring our trainees to reflect 'deliberately' on learning at each stage. They were encouraged to take part, to post at least one message at each of the five levels, to contribute to the 'reflections' conferences, to complete their exit questionnaires – and only then to ask for their certificate of completion, training payments and expenses.

The training programme was developed and updated year by year. By 1999, over 400 trainees had taken part, with nearly all commenting on their experience of the training through the reflections conferences and exit questionnaires. We also monitored the work of the e-moderators with their students and made adjustments to the training. The examples that follow are from version five, the 1999 version of the online training in OUBS.

OUBS training programme

We base the five levels of the online training on the five-stage model described in Chapter 2, Figure 2.1. At every level, the simplest possible set of instructions accompanies activities in the online environment. The printed booklet accompanying the training programme offers a list of conferences to aid navigation, copies of what the screen should look like to the trainee at various stages and a print-out of key online instructions, eg how to post a CV (résumé), how to send messages.

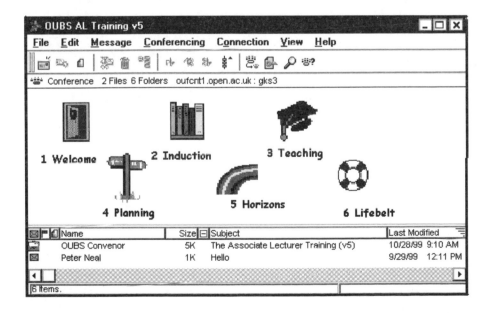

Figure 4.1 *Desktop screen of online training in OUBS*

When a trainee logs on, she or he sees five icons, representing the five levels of the training programme. In addition, Lifebelt (or help) icon is available which contains virus prevention software, downloadable manuals, FAQs about the software, Code of Practice for use of the system, helpdesk phone numbers and even a 'lifeguard' to e-mail if necessary.

This is our first message to trainees:

WELCOME!

Each stage will offer you skills with a range of activities designed to enable you to practice those skills. For the early stages the programme will give you quite a lot of help, but for the final stages it will only give limited guidance. By the end of the programme you should have the skills required to work with your students in a productive way.

It is strongly recommended that you work through one stage before moving on to the next. Please visit the 'Reflections' conference at each level before closing that level and moving on to the next. We will use these for evaluating the training and research into conferencing.

Aims and objectives of this training programme

The aims of the programme are to:

- provide you with the technical skills to access and use the FirstClass system and to undertake a range of tasks online;
- provide you with the experience and confidence to use the FirstClass system as a key resource in teaching and learning online as an AL;
- enable you to become an active member of the OUBS online community, participating in and contributing to School, programme and course conferences.

The introductory message for each of the five stages in the training explains the purpose of that stage. Now click on the Welcome icon and announce your arrival! OUBS Convenor

Level one: Welcome

The purpose of this level is to ensure that trainees can find a conference, find, read and send messages, discover who else is taking part and give a little information about themselves.

The new trainee's first task is to visit the 'arrivals' conference, where they find instructions on posting a simple message to announce their arrival. Most trainees succeed in achieving this task on their first, or sometimes their second, log-in. However, their relief or jubilation at having 'made it' is often obvious:

At last!! It has been a long struggle. BT

Signing in and completely new to the OU. Look forward to learning a lot from your experiences. JO

Just made it here myself. . . it's my first go at any of this. Looking forward to really arriving (that is, having a good handle on the system). EM

I was preparing to sneak in by the back door but feel so much better having spotted several other 'started before but life got in the way' messages. JI

I have used FirstClass before, as a student, and I thought it was BRILLIANT. But have not used it recently and now as a tutor, am a bit apprehensive about actually e-moderating conferences. JS

I have arrived but not sure if I have landed – if you know what I mean! PP

Present but probably not correct! DB

Ho there – my first action is to print everything because I can't remember anything but the fact that I can't remember anything and have to do something creative to cope – like printing a whole load of instructions. RM

These efforts are rewarded by a personal 'congratulations and welcome' message from the online trainer (whom we call convenor in this context). At this stage the convenor will also point the new trainee to any sources of help and attempt to assuage any worries or grievances. Many trainees remember the importance of their individual welcome into the online environment when questioned months or even years later, so we feel it is always worthwhile.

At Level one we also invite trainees to explore the difference between e-mail and conferencing. Increasingly, trainee e-moderators are presenting with fairly well developed e-mail skills. It is important to explain the differences to build on their prior knowledge and expertise. Finally we explain how to look at the résumés of other participants in the training, and invite them to post their own. We emphasize the important of posting a few details about oneself early in the training, since we have found that every participant feels more comfortable if right from the start, they have a little knowledge about people they are working with.

Finally, the last task at Level one is to post a message to reflect on their experiences so far. Here is our invitation message:

Reflections on Level one

Please ensure that you have completed all the tasks at this level. Then send a message to this conference reflecting on:

The key learning points from your initial experiences in the training.
After you have completed your reflections message, please close all the windows from Level 1, and click onto Level 2 Induction' (the bookshelf icon). OUBS Convenor

Most participants respond, establishing, we think, a small amount of reflection from the start of their journey into conference e-moderation. Here are some examples of their messages:

> Things often look simple, and can also be simplified, but below the surface there's a lot more than meets the eye. TD
>
> Hey, this isn't so bad. I thought it would be much more complicated given my not so literate computer skills! AL
>
> My overwhelming sense of achievement at leaving this message is diminished by the entirely predictable instability of virtual communications. I feel like I've been trying to send smoke signals in a force 9 wind. DB

Level two: Induction

Level two, equivalent to stage two in the model, enables trainees to learn about protocols and how to relate to others through this medium, and to acquire useful software skills.

Trainees work through exercises aimed at analyzing a mock discussion among students who are conferencing about a television programme. The 'participants' are making all the classic mistakes (lack of titles to messages, advertising, messages in the wrong conference, failure to re-title messages when replying and changing topics, 'parental responses' rather than collegiate and attempts at domination of the discussion). The discussion has a 'real' (virtual) feel about it. Trainees are invited to view each message and consider how well or otherwise it contributes to the discussion. Feedback suggests that this is a very successful exercise for trainee e-moderators.

One trainee found this exercise particularly helpful:

> I think this exercise is an excellent one for its richness. It has a provocative title to get you into it, but sorting out the 'good' from the 'bad' proves a little too difficult for me. I would rather view it as an interesting insight into the different motivations these students may have for using online conferencing. On the other hand almost all the participants could be prompted to keep brushing up their netiquette! Great learning, thanks. ML

In addition, trainees are invited to explore appropriate communication styles online by sending a 'postcard'. We have found that this simple metaphor enables trainees to practise giving straightforward information in short messages. It also results in some sharing of information about themselves and some fun!

Here is our message:

Send us a postcard, please!

It takes time to develop a style of your own online – usually somewhere between writing and speaking. It needs to be brief – more than one screenful is rarely appropriate, but informative without being indecipherable or offensive to anyone who might read it. This is not meant to put you off in any way!

Some people suggest that writing conference messages is a bit like writing a postcard. This is your chance to try it!

Use this conference to send a message to your colleague of maximum one screenful. This could give some information about you, or perhaps seek information from others. OUBS Convenor

The postcard messages offer fascinating insights into our trainees, who typically mention their location and often why they're working online instead of doing something else!

As I sit here on a Friday evening in dark decided wintry Brussels I can imagine the perfect golfing day – warm and sunny with a little breeze. Never mind for those of you who know Brussels you will know this scene is sadly a very rare actual occurrence – but it has the benefit that you are not often distracted in reality! 'Au revoir' and 'bon weekend'. Best regards. KD

The beauty of this postcard for me is that I don't have to hunt around for a stamp! Usually I forget to buy them. Here in Hampton (West London) it's a glorious sunny morning – postcard weather even. Just off to the Tate Gallery for a cultural fix and then a look at the Millennium Wheel on the South Bank – I've seen it in the horizontal position and now I want to see the vertical version. Regards PB

Not sure 'I wish you were here' in my study staring at a VDU. Life is for living – can you be living focused at a screen, yes I know 'virtual reality' is supposed to be the answer. Can you really experience life by accessing a screen? EP

Fellow holiday-makers, I am sitting here in rainy Dublin, the Celtic tiger looks more like a drowned rat and I am faced with the familiar dilemma of what spurious candyfloss I can use to fill the blank space of a post card. Missing you already AN

Trainees visit the reflection conference at Level two before they move on, which asks:

What key learning points from your progress on the training so far would you pass on to your students?

Here is an example response:

> Amazingly enough it's all beginning to fall into place. My confidence in using FirstClass (which I have never used before) is increasing rapidly and I'm not so scared of pressing the wrong button. I have learnt a lot about setting up conferences and keeping them going etc. I find that the contributions from others online, both experienced and new ones, is really useful as there is a wealth of experience out there. This would be my advice to my students – try it – it's amazing! Thanks. FH

Level three: Teaching

Level three, equivalent to stage three in the model, is concerned with giving and receiving information. We have found that trainees like to gain and share information around their professional task of teaching online. We also focus on exercises that show them how to set up their own online conferences. We include an essential practice area, and we offer exercises and discussions on the role of the e-moderator including practice in opening conferences and the 'weaving' of conference messages together. Trainees are invited to post examples of their own opening messages and to comment on those of their fellow trainees.

Trainees visit the reflections conference before exiting Level three, and again we ask them:

> What key learning points from your progress on the training so far would you pass on to colleagues from a teaching perspective?

By this stage, some excitement and trepidation about conferencing 'for real' is occurring, but there is also evidence of some real learning. Here are some examples of Level three reflections. One participant details his new insights into e-moderating:

> **Lurking**
> I agree that lurking (still looking for a more neutral term) needs investigating as colleagues suggest but note that you can check who has read a message by going to 'History'. This may allow you to identify those who are not picking up the messages (e.g. in a tutorial group) which might justify a phone call. The person may have technical problems, or may be looking in the wrong place. Still lurking is better than not participating at all!
>
> **Weaving**
> HP certainly sums it up well for me: you do have the option of setting up another sub-conference so those who want to wander off can do so in parallel with the main topic in hand. Summarizing the main points so far that are on track and adding a few pertinent questions would also help. I

LITTLEHAMPTON BOOK SERVICES LTD.

Faraday Close – Durrington
West Sussex – BN13 3RB

Tel: (01903) 828800
Fax: (01903) 828801

** INVOICE **
Credit Card With Order

CUSTOMER VAT NUMBER A

LBS VAT NUMBER

GB 620 5837 52

Banker:

Barclays Bank PLC
54 Lombard Street
London
EC3V 9EX

Account No: 30402842
Bank Code: 20-00-00
Girobank No: 516 6152
Page 1

DELIVER TO

MR D GRAY
University of Strathclyde
Jordanhill Campus
76 Southbrae Drive
Glasgow
Lanarkshire   G13 1PP

FOR THE ATTENTION OF

FOR ONWARD SHIPMENT TO

AA612452

INVOICE ADDRESS

MR D GRAY
University of Strathclyde
Jordanhill Campus
76 Southbrae Drive
Glasgow
Lanarkshire   G13 1PP

ACCOUNT No

10041630

INVOICE OR CREDIT No

52929809

DATE

17-01-01

DESPATCHED METHOD

Royal Mail

DESPATCH ROUTE

Inland Post

Quantity	ISBN	Order Ref/Title Details	HB/PB	Pub	Disc%	Trade	Trade

				Price	Value
1	0749431105	408714/01/01 E-Moderating: Teach & Learn Online	PB	18.99	15.2000	15.20
	POSTAGE				1.52

If your order attracts postage this will be included in total invoice cost item recorded will be held until book is available or the order cancelled se note your Credit Card has been charged to the value of this invoice. I have any quries contact Mail Order on 01903 828503 or fax 01903 828623, qu this invoice number.

Payment Received With Thanks.

. Any
. Plea
f you
oting

TOTAL	16.72
TAX	
TOTAL	16.72

| TOTAL QTY. | 1 | TOTAL WEIGHT | 0.296 |

Sterling

guess one of the best preparations for a flagging discussion is to keep a few things up your sleeve, so that if/when things flag you have something new/interesting to add in to give it a boost.

Summarizing

I will need to be more encouraging about the contributions individually, select a title that would stand out more to enable late comers to catch up without having to read all the 'red flags' and end with a question if I were 'going live'. Wouldn't you agree. . . ? J. :-) JS

Other trainees compare e-moderating to facilitating face-to-face groups:

For me, opening, weaving, e-modding are, in many ways, just like getting a discussion going in a face-to-face setting. The skills required are the same, only the medium is a little different. Someone once told me that an online discussion group is much like having a party in a dark living room. No one can see one another, but everyone hears what is being said. There are those who whisper in the corners (go off-conference, 1-to-1 e-mail) where others can't hear, but for the most part, one can only make sense of what is going on by paying good attention. This may be a dying art – and there are times I believe that. Enjoy FM

I think conferencing can be a valuable learning tool – capturing immediate reactions and ideas, which are often, very stimulating and which often get lost in assignments and face-to-face seminars – a virtual learning organization! AA

Level four: Knowledge construction

Level four is equivalent to stage four of the model. We have found that stimulating trainees to discuss how they will use CMC with their students works best at this level. We provide a discussion forum so that trainees can 'meet' and 'discuss' issues with those from their own course or programme. We also attach some texts for them to consider. This gives practice in downloading attached documents as well as giving them ideas to explore. As always a reflections conference is provided at this level to encourage them to consider their progress. They are asked this time:

How do you feel about working with Computer Mediated Conferencing (CMC) with your students, based on your experience of the training so far?

Trainees recognize that they need to get real experience in working with students:

I feel confident enough to get started, but am fully aware I will continue to learn, and probably learn a lot, through actual doing. BF

I feel quite comfortable with this. I used the old CoSy conferencing in my student days and absolutely loved it. It was really helpful in my studies and a very useful contact with other students (especially those on the same course but not necessarily in my tutor group), and other tutors other than my own. It gave me a far broader view than I would ever have achieved otherwise. I hope I can pass this enthusiasm on to my students, and get as many of them as possible involved in using computer conferencing as part of their studies. I guess central to this will be my role in providing the right environment in the conference for lively and useful discussion and support for novice users, so that they can see a real advantage in using it. JB

I've derived great benefit from reading everybody else's reflections. It has truly widened my appreciation not only of the potential of the medium but also of its role in teaching and learning online. I'm ready and raring to do it for real but realize that I will need to 'stand back' and encourage the knowledge flow. JH

I've found computer conferencing an easy and effective method of engaging in debate as a student. Having completed this training I am about to find out what it is like on the other side of the modem as a tutor! I'm determined to build a sense of community with my group and perhaps encourage those who are less willing to contribute face-to-face to do so over the electronic system. (I wonder, however, just how intimidating it is for those who are not as computer literate as I am?) I'll have to ask my group. JP

Level five: Development

This level is equivalent to stage five of the model. Here we explore the use of the Web in teaching, both to build up to trainees' confidence and enable them to consider how they might embed Web resources in their own e-moderating. Trainees share their favourite search engines and sites for their discipline.

The exit questionnaire provides simple feedback to us about the trainees' experience of the whole programme and has enabled us to make incremental adjustments and improvements over the years. Quantitative and qualitative feedback from the exit questionnaire helps us to confirm and develop the exercises and approaches throughout the five levels. Trainees very consistently confirm that the five-stage model of training works for them. Creating motivation at Level one is probably the most complex challenge along with the encouragement of trainees to keep working through each of the levels until they reach Level five. However, from Level two onwards, confidence grows in almost every trainee and many are very appreciative of learning or reinforcing online communication skills and information exchange at Levels two and three. Several comment that these are basic life and business skills that are not otherwise taught in this way. At Level four, trainees really appreciate the focus on e-moderating and considerable anticipation is generated. By Level five, nearly all trainees are very keen indeed to try out their new skills on their participants!

The vast majority of trainees appreciate the highly structured, staged approach to training and learning software and e-moderating skills in an integrated way. A small minority, however, continues to ask for a software 'manual'. They often express this as an 'idiot's' guide to the system. Regrettably, it is not easy for us to simplify an interactive and complex system sufficiently for these people. We encourage such groups to download the instructions that they seek. Another small minority is happy with the training programme taking place entirely online, but wish to take their own route through the training exercises and conferences. We allow for this, of course, although we do find that a lower percentage of this group completes the programme.

Most concerns are somewhat alleviated by the time trainees complete the programme and most consider investment in their training 'good value' for the use of their previous time. However, those worries that remain are typically about the use of their time when working online with students, suggesting that expectations, reward and recognition in the use of e-moderating time must always be given careful consideration.

> I have two fears: 1) my students not using it very much; and 2) it will be used a lot by my students and it will take up too much time! MD
>
> Some students may be accessing conferences through an employer's system at no phone cost to them. Could this encourage excessive inputs and unreasonable demands on the e-moderator's time? PB
>
> And a word of caution. It all gets so engrossing that it is easy to forget the phone bill or that it is way past bedtime again! People at the office will be wondering why I always seem so tired. NH

Most trainees feel they have achieved and accomplished personal development by Level five and are very pleased to have completed the programme. Completing trainees frequently say they believe such a training programme should be compulsory for e-moderators before they are 'let loose' on student conferences. They express very tangible progress compared to their first tentative messages at Level one. Some are by then already working with their students online. Some are very enthusiastic:

> This is the future. I have seen it and it works (sometimes). BA
>
> Using CMC reminds me of the time I learnt to drive a car, I was very proud I could drive, but now I am much more interested in the places I can visit in the car. I have a feeling this is going to be similar. HF

Monitoring the work of trained e-moderators

The Open University has always had policies and extensive systems to monitor the quality of its tutors' performance. It provides them with feedback and offers development where necessary. Until the advent of large-scale CMC, this monitoring took the form of visits to face-to-face tutorials, day schools and residential schools by full time academic staff, and the systematic and very large scale monitoring of correspondence tuition, based on a peer review system. Drawing on the experience and procedures for these, we devised and implemented from February 1996 a system of monitoring of online e-moderation of CMC for the Business School. This system involves a series of virtual 'visits' to each conference by peer or colleague tutors who have fully and successfully completed the online training. They provide reports on their view of conferences that they visit and comment whenever they find good practice in e-moderation. They also alert managers to problems or lack of participation. There is a direct correlation between active e-moderation and successful completion of the online training. The monitoring system has been gradually built up and refined over the past few years, and is now extending to other courses and faculties.

An online community of OUBS tutors has also emerged, centred on discussion and information conferences known as the 'SCR' (Senior Common Room). The exchange of good practice, support, collaboration – and the flattening of communications with the full time course team – are welcome. We did not anticipate the importance and strength of these communications devices at first but they have proved an unexpected bonus. There is little doubt that the training has produced new cohorts of OUBS tutors comfortable with communicating electronically. This has an almost immeasurable impact on the sense of professional community that this generated. I recommend to everyone that they set up an easily accessed but 'e-moderators only' online conference for sharing and exploring good practice.

To gradually build up appropriate and consistent e-moderating practice in your own context, you do need to set up monitoring of your e-moderators' work. You may, like us, wish to base this on a peer review system. It is tempting to revert to visiting face-to-face sessions, where these are feasible, but it is better to review and monitor the work of e-moderators online. I suggest you make sure that the reviewers are fully comfortable and competent themselves as e-moderators, so they don't apply old paradigms of teaching and learning to the new environment! Of course, another important way of determining the success of the work of the e-moderators is to explore the responses of the participants. Chapter 5 provides some ideas for success factors for participants.

This chapter has explained and explored preparing and training for e-moderation. The following Resources for practitioners will help you create training programmes for your e-moderators:

Chapter 5

E-moderators and the participants' experience

This chapter focuses on understanding the participants' experiences of CMC. E-moderators could fall into the trap of thinking of CMC as one experience, whereas each participant will respond according to his or her individual needs. In this chapter I explore, with case studies and examples, the needs of special groups such as novices to computing and people with disabilities as well as attempting to explain some CMC behaviours such as 'lurking'.

Frequently, participants' expectations of online learning are high, but some become disillusioned and disengaged. The support and actions of e-moderators, more than the functions of the technology in use, can truly make the difference between disappointment and highly productive learning. I suggest that as an e-moderator you should imagine what it is like to be a novice participant. I mean you should try to put yourself in the shoes (or at the keyboards) of your participants. In this way, you will be aware of the barriers that prevent learning, as well as discovering how to include every member of your online group.

Access and participation

Participants' readiness to learn online is the first issue e-moderators need to consider. Rheingold articulates well the novice's fears:

> Fear is an important element in every novice computer user's first attempts to use a new machine or new software: fear of destroying data, fear of hurting the machine, fear of seeming stupid in comparison to other users, or even to the machine itself. (Rheingold, 1995: 10).

It is so easy for us, used to working online, to forget what it's like to be a novice. My colleague at the Open University Business School, Ken Giles, now one of the most experienced e-moderators I know, recalls how he felt when first confronted with working through CMC:

> I'm not really fundamentally interested in computers as such. I just want to use the technology in the same way I use a telephone to achieve results that matter to me, that is, I want the system to take care of itself and not require too much precise intervention by me. When I admire ducks swimming on a pond, I'm not much concerned with what's going on under the water. I can still remember vividly what it was like to be a novice! Well, you need keyboarding skills before you can use Windows. My own way in was that I knew where the keyboard letters were because I could type (with two fingers). I didn't know a great deal about Windows (but just about enough to get started with CMC). And so had problems initially with things like downloading (I couldn't find where stuff went!), screen sizing, opening and closing windows. The first hurdle was installing the software and getting connected. When you're on your own and not very confident, setting up a remote connection can be a major hurdle. Unfortunately, the nature of the beast is such that a pragmatist like me can't just dive in and have a bash. 'I wonder what will happen if I do this. . .' usually doesn't work! Get one thing wrong in the sequence of steps, even a misplaced dot, and that means trouble — trouble for someone who already feels anxious about the process. Too often, even today, I'm aware I complete information requested in splash screens without really understanding the implications and I get things wrong as a result. Ignorance is not bliss, but I don't really want to bother with acquiring such understanding. And when you've got over the initial hurdles of getting connected, there's the worry that through ignorance you'll do something silly that will show you up publicly — send a message to the whole world by mistake, or wipe something out that's crucial. And all this with the speed of someone not well trained in keyboarding skills. . . and perhaps concerned about online telephone cost. . . I could go on. . . but you know, it was all worth it in the end. Ken.

The relatively few 'early adopters' are likely to tolerate technology that does not always work and be willing to take risks — they will believe that the benefits outweigh the difficulties (Norman, 1999). However, most CMC participants fall into the 95 per cent category of late or later adopters of the technology. These people will be pragmatic and realistic, looking for convenience and reliability, and their tolerance will be low. Most will not want their learning to be disrupted. Would you?

Putman (1991) in commenting on reflective practice, points out that new users search for rules and recipes early in the learning process. The best way to help them is to offer a start, then 'stand back' and gradually let the user embed the learning in his or own experience.

Prior success or failure can be crucial. Rogers describes a 'test' that adults use when deciding how easy or difficult it will be to learn something new:

how far the subject matter coincides with what the individual believes to be their own abilities. Usually built on prior experience of success/satisfaction or failure, the perception of personal attributes will to a large extent determine the location of the subject matter in proximity to or remoteness from the self. (Rogers, 1993: 205).

In the early stages of learning CMC, users draw on their previous computing experience if they have any. In most contexts, the percentages of students with difficulties over access or with no computing knowledge are decreasing. This trend is likely to continue. However, students' experience is most often in word processing or spreadsheeting, surfing the Internet for information or in playing multimedia games. As yet, few students are starting to learn through CMC with much experience of communicating through computers. Training and induction programmes will be important for some years to come.

Even those participants who are very familiar and comfortable with e-mail need some support in understanding the collaborative and collegiate environments offered by conferencing. Some students need help with appreciating the shift in the teaching and learning approach that accompanies increased use of CMC. In stage one in the five-stage model there is a strong element of deferred gratification. As participants are struggling to get their hardware, software and links set up, the benefits may not be intrinsically obvious to them! Their expectations of what the e-moderator can and will offer are often very high.

Skills that are promoted and developed through CMC may well be important study and work skills for the future. Participants need to become literate in online communication: this is going back to writing and reading, involving extensive use of typed text. They need to develop new skills of acquiring and managing information and knowledge obtained in the online environment – and applied elsewhere. Learners need the ability to select items from masses of data to inform their judgements. They need to learn flexibility in using varied resources. They need to function in global communities. They need to maintain their motivation without constantly meeting in learning groups, and without encountering the professor in the corridor. While induction into CMC will not meet all these needs at a stroke, it can lay the foundation for the development of such skills.

CMC technology will in due course become widely available, and computer use will doubtless be taken for granted like the telephone. For some novices, meantime, the potential benefits of CMC may only be readily accessible with careful support.

To learn effectively once a course begins, CMC novices need to feel comfortable in the medium first, during their pre-course induction and training. In learning computing skills, two main types of knowledge are needed. These are 'declarative knowledge' or 'facts' (eg what icons exist on the screen), and 'procedural knowledge' (eg how to undertake tasks with the keyboard or mouse). In learning to undertake a series of tasks such as those involved in CMC, learners need to memorize basic sequences and gradually build up associations with prior knowledge before starting to undertake these procedures almost automatically, as they do when driving a vehicle. Then they can hope to benefit from CMC's collaborative learning potential.

Induction needs to be planned, to take account of novices' need to learn the skills and procedures of the software, and how to operate in CMC successfully and productively. My own experience leads me to think that this induction requires a staged but extensive process, to be undertaken online rather than through more traditional teaching or training.

Learning styles and approaches

All e-moderators need to develop a clear sense of their 'audience', however, as well as of the purposes of groups whose work they are facilitating in the online environment. When e-moderating online it is easy to have a standard image in your mind of 'the students', but the best e-moderators manage to keep a sense of the composite needs of the group, along with those of a variety of individuals.

CMC must be tailored to appeal to all learning styles to avoid the need for offering a variety of learning methods. Teachers in the classroom respond to differing styles through working with individuals. Similarly, e-moderators should be responsive to individuals' needs online, rather than assuming that the only way to deal with individuals is to revert to meeting face to face.

In face-to-face groups, most communication involves talking and listening so those students who learn aurally are well accommodated. However, CMC occurs through reading and writing. It is likely therefore that it will appeal to those more comfortable with the written word. This places at a disadvantage those for whom writing (or typing) is a problem, or who are working in something other than their first language. In the OU Business School, we accommodate large numbers of students working through CMC who are using English but it is not their first language. Typically they prefer to read and compose offline and take their time. They also need reassurance that minor mistakes are made by everyone in conference messages and so long as the sense is clear, this is unimportant.

Honey and Mumford (1986) suggest that students use a mixture of active, practical, theoretical and reflective learning. Activists, as they call their first category, tend to learn best when they are dealing with new problems and experiences. These learners need to have a range of different activities to keep them engaged, and the ability to 'hold the floor' (or in this context, the conference) and to be able to 'bounce ideas' off of others, all of which CMC caters for extremely well. Pragmatists, on the other hand, need to be able to see an obvious link between what they are learning and problems or opportunities with which they are engaged in their work. They must become fully engaged in the learning process. They tend to want an immediate opportunity to try out what they have learnt in order to evaluate its practical use and value. In designing CMC, pragmatists can be catered for through online activities. Honey and Mumford's theorists need suffi-cient time to explore the links between ideas and situations. As the asynchronous nature of CMC builds in a time delay and, with structure and encouragement, the exploration can occur. The high level of peer interaction in CMC should appeal to theorists, although they are likely to be the first to cry, 'it's all rubbish' if topics are not dealt with in depth. Good structure and archiving are important, so they can work in appropriate conferences with serious topics. E-moderators should, as always, encourage questioning, probing and exploring.

Honey and Mumford's reflectors probably benefit most from CMC. They engage with the learning task with time to think deeply about the concepts and activities, and to give considered responses that synchronicity and conventional classrooms rarely allow. Experienced e-moderators such as Gerry Prendergast from Abacus Virtual College suggested to me that activists and pragmatists frequently behave online as if they were extrovert personalities, while the theorists and reflectors have more introverted styles.

E-moderators need to keep these various styles in mind and plan their CMC accordingly. In particular, a clear mixture of engagement in immediately relevant activities, and the opportunity to reflect on messages or eventually contribute some, are both important. Activities can either be entirely online, begun face-to-face and extended online, or prepared for online and continued face-to-face. An array of tasks can be provided and groups can be split into smaller learning sets. Such variations are likely to meet a wide variety of learning styles and preferences.

Disabilities and CMC

In the United Kingdom more than 4 per cent of students have an acknowledged disability and true numbers are probably closer to 10 per cent (Newell, 1999). At the OU, 7,000 students declare a disability and 1,000 of these prefer other than print materials. In some countries, legislation requires at least minimum access to courseware for disabled learners. What can CMC do for them? Is it accessible?

In CMC the messages appear to others as an individual's thoughts, without them knowing much at all about the writer's age, race, appearance, gender and disability (Gold, 1998). Users with a disability appreciate that they can use CMC more or less at any time and in any place, obviating the need for travel and physical access. Instead, they are valued for their thoughts and contributions. The challenge for you as an e-moderator is to be aware of the issues involved. Valuing every contribution is essential. Doing so is likely to engender the best possible response from anyone who is disadvantaged, whatever the reason.

CMC can be an open door for those with restricted mobility or difficulty in accessing buildings. CMC provides an opportunity to 'travel', meet and learn with others with comparative ease, but only if accessible materials and processes are on offer. Technology can help or hinder, of course. Keyboard or speech commands can be provided for those unable to use a mouse. Electronic text can be designed so that it converts to Braille. With forethought, Web pages can be designed to be more effective for certain disabilities although the increased emphasis on graphics has created new challenges, especially for smaller providers of software packages.

A visually impaired tutor took part in the online e-moderator training (see Chapter 4) and appeared on my first list of 'lurkers' to follow up by telephone. I discovered he was waiting for special software to be installed and was meanwhile having the messages read to him. He soon secured software that produced an audio version of FirstClass and took part later in the training with very few problems. He proved to be an effective and active e-moderator on OU Business School conferences. The learning point for me here was that I should not assume lurking necessarily meant laziness – participating might take longer for some people with visual impairment, but they can still gain and contribute.

Blind participants can adapt CMC software through Braille printouts of messages or through using speech synthesis. They cannot use a mouse so need to become adept at keyboard commands. An experienced intermediary is needed to train and support blind users to the point of competence and independence. When changes are made to the system, blind participants must be notified early so that they can arrange for specific adaptations and training, in advance. Manuals and instructions need to be recorded onto audio tape by experienced readers able to describe flow chart diagrams and the like, in words.

In constructing conferences, consider the font and style and how they might look on a variety of screens and to different people. This will help those with partial visual impairment, but will also be of benefit to all users. Even where course texts are provided as print, it can be helpful also to provide them electronically, so that visually impaired users can manipulate fonts, sizes and styles to suit their personal needs. The Open University puts some of its courses onto CD ROM so that they can be played with a speech synthesizer, or displayed as larger print: the CD ROMs carry a voice-recording too.

A deaf colleague wrote to me on e-mail of his encounters with CMC:

> Conferencing was for me a hugely liberating experience. I started working in industry in 1973, when the 'managerial communications' model was through using the telephone. My then MD was someone of good heart and intentions who thought I would never be able to 'be a manager' because I was excluded from the information community of the company. Not his terms but that's what he meant. So I was placed into special projects, away in an alcove, where I could work on my own.
>
> I arrived at the OU in 1986 just as the CoSy conferencing system was getting implemented. It was a secret known to a few – I heard about it by grapevine over the photocopier. I joined and nothing was the same again.
>
> Liberation came for me in several linked forms. Firstly was the sense of 'connectedness' – the world expanded beyond my desk. I didn't have to get up and physically see someone in order to make contact. The relief from a sense of embattled isolation was immense. Second was the increased meaning in communications because I could find out more about the context of what was going on. Not just answer a specific question but get

a sense of why some things were seen as problems or opportunities. That meant having a 'relatively' relaxed sense of the 'social' or off-topic communications that frame the on-topic discussions. This is quite important in giving a sense of communicative competence.

Third is another aspect of communicative competence. The ability to 'say'. This can be difficult for deaf people as communication face-to-face needs an awareness of the social turn-taking codes of communications and these can be very subtle. Hesitate and you are excluded. So conferencing can unleash the power of 'speech' for a deaf person. It did a lot for my confidence in other situations too.

Here is where an e-moderator can play a part, by fostering an appropriate online communication code so that all can find a way to take turns.

A factor that didn't apply for me but does for other deaf people (especially for those whose first language is signing) is that literacy can be a problem. English can be very much the second language for some people and written English a particular trial. So conferencing isn't necessarily a panacea for the deaf... Maybe some awareness by e-moderators of strange and sudden pitfalls with written language can help.

Finally conferencing – and associated e-mail facilities – puts the initiative with a deaf person. Not being dependent on others to initiate or negotiate contacts is once again a liberating experience. Freedom can be rather frightening, so for me the e-moderator's role in creating 'safe spaces' is very important.

(Bevan, 1999)

Online educational counselling for learners with long-term health problems can be provided using CMC for social and study support within the environment of a peer group area accessible only to specified participants. Margaret Debenham suggests recruiting two e-moderators. One (from the student group) looks after chat, medical and technical discussion issues, leaving the educational counsellor as e-moderator of an educational support topic. Margaret tells us that CMC fosters communication with the participants, which is both 'intimate and distancing', as well as promoting a considered dialogue between counsellor and student. In her study, the participants demonstrated increased motivation towards their studies and the majority preferred support online to the support through the telephone (Debenham *et al.*, 1999).

University of Maryland University College case study

Claudine SchWeber of the University of Maryland University College, outside Washington, DC, who has experience of e-moderating in innovative ways, sees e-moderating as 'guiding a discussion and fostering interaction among students rather than between students and instructors.' This can be a challenge, because as Dr SchWeber points out, the tendency in a question and answer session online, much like some onsite classes, is for the students to respond to the instructor rather than to each other. The Maryland experience suggests the importance of purposeful and explorative nature of collaborative working online. The best activity was through an online case analysis where students commented, reacted and referred to each other's work. This case study shows how potentially contentious and emotive issues can be surfaced and explored productively online through supportive groups.

The key e-moderating activity in this example was setting up appropriate and challenging questions to ask online and the gradual sequencing and release of appropriate material. The case dealt with an engineering company's branch located in the West Indies, far away from the headquarters somewhere in Europe. It involved issues of management and supervision, superior and subordinate relations, race, age, perception, organizational culture, feedback, trust, diversity, feedback, new and experienced staff, home country and expatriate relations – and a surprise ending. What a great way of gradually introducing material into an asynchronous environment! They started out with four guiding questions on which students were asked to comment by a given date:

1. What are the perceptual issues? How did these impact the situation and affect the outcome?
2. What are the cultural/diversity issues? How did these affect the relationship between B and R, and R to the rest of the unit?
3. What are the performance appraisal and retention issues? What motivational and job satisfaction issues played a role here? How might B have handled the situation if he knew about relevant management theory?
4. What are the trust, communication, and feedback issues here? What strategies did the men ignore? What might have been done? Then, the question that brought it home: assume Y has been fired and you have been brought in to replace him. What might you do in the next two weeks? Why?

Even before the due date, the class became intensively involved in the questions and in what they might do as a replacement for Y. Some of the students were originally from countries outside of the United States and from ethnic and racial minorities. Their reaction to the expatriates and locals situation in the case was intense, highly engaged and from their personal perspective, as these excerpts show:

Trust was an issue from the very beginning. As I am a (member of) minority myself, I am glad that X left the company. I wish he had done it sooner. I did see it coming though. What gives anyone the right to imply that they know a race of people without ever walking in that race's shoes?

Our views, while similar in affront (for the most part), differ when it comes to agreeing with R's decision. Under the circumstances it would be difficult not to share his anger. I still believe, however, that he blew it.

On your question 'What gives anyone the right to imply that they know a race of people without ever walking in that race shoes' – how do you feel about X's written comments 'bashing' (others)? And, you made several comments about the expatriates, suggesting they all behaved like Y. The case study gives no evidence of this.

The online discussion, commentary, reaction and referrals went on for about a week, as those who joined in later got involved in some section of the comments. Dr SchWeber pointed out that this had never, ever occurred in a face-to-face class; not with the same intensity, not with that frequency of response to each other (several people made several comments), not in the students' willingness to disagree (as noted above) on controversial topics such as race, nor in their apparent ability to look at the conceptual issues and the theory that might apply.

One dramatic difference from the face-to-face class was that there was an ongoing CMC transcript, so students could join in at any point and comment on points made earlier (which they did), or refer to each other's recommendations. For example, one student said, 'A's recommendation to hire J as a consultant is a good point because. . . '. That kept the dialogue going, somewhat like a ball on an elastic that keeps bouncing back in and going out again. Dr SchWeber eventually met the students and when the case was brought up, everyone was much more subdued and discussion did not take much time. Faculty colleagues who looked in later on the discussion on CMC said that they had never seen such a fine and thorough discussion of this particular case.

Corporate training and development

Top management is increasingly realizing that their access to the Internet is critical. In 1991 it was estimated that only 13 per cent of top executives in Japan, 9 per cent in the United Kingdom, 7 per cent in Germany and 3 per cent in France had access to the Internet. Surely every senior manager in these countries now has access? Could this be the new competitive capacity issue?

The research on which this book is based was conducted with distance learning students on a programme leading to a qualification, the MBA. However, in these times of major emphasis on life-long learning, 'learning organizations' and 'corporate universities', the role of CMC for corporate education is becoming increasingly important (Schreiber and Berge, 1998). CMC is especially useful for organizations where many employees are distributed across different geographical locations or travel frequently as the online environment can be used to productively share knowledge and create a joint sense of mission. Much of the advice given in Part 2, Resources for practitioners, especially relating to access, e-moderator training, good online design and the purposeful nature of each and every conference, hold good. However, careful consideration needs to be given by the e-moderator to the structure and form of participation of online groupings and to building of trust in communications, especially if learning groups cross formal organizational boundaries and hierarchies.

If you are considering a learning site with CMC within an executive development programme, you need to be especially sensitive to the sub-cultures within which managers and executives typically operate. Executives are usually comfortable with information as holistic, complex and imprecise and they may especially value learning from peers. They frequently feel isolated and remote in their role and often find themselves in only formal relationships with immediate work groups. They often relate best to peers within their industry but outside their own organization. They are likely to see IT as limiting and distorting and their fear of 'failure' in its use may be very high. In some sectors, senior managers rely on secretarial or administrative support and therefore lack online experience. The audience for your online learning programmes may be transitional due to especially high mobility. The need for early and useful learning outcomes is critical. For these kinds of programmes, e-moderators need to work even harder than usual to integrate the online learning with other activities and to ensure authentic and relevant CMC activities.

There is a feeling in commercial organizations that the investment that universities are making in IT is lagging behind that of the corporate environment (Robinson et al., 1998). They often, however, assume that a learner, familiar with business processes online, will be as comfortable with learning online. My experience is that this is not the case. In addition, there is still little understanding of how in-company learning systems link effectively with aspiring knowledge management processes and systems and in particular how one feeds the other. Induction programmes into the online learning environment, preferably with good in-company support, are therefore especially critical to success.

Gender and e-moderating

Very recently, access by women to networked computers, has reached a similar level to that by men. Some authorities believe that women's ways of communicating and working lend themselves particularly happily to CMC (Lapham, 1998) and that 'all girls need modems!' (from Rosie Scott, who started Geek Girl). Women are generally perceived to be comfortable with communications technologies such as the telephone but, because of the somewhat male-orientated image of computers, may be initially put off CMC. Telephones ensure a one-to-one conversation, but CMC involves group behaviour and much depends on the e-moderation of the group. E-moderators need therefore to concentrate on focusing on individuals' contributions to conferences, rather than their offline gender or identity.

Others are concerned that online discussions may be dominated in some of the same ways that occur in face-to-face groups. Spender's (1995) book gives a wide exploration of the issues of women, communications and computers. As she points out:

> One of the starting points for change has to be in the educational arena. For more than a century, women have been engaged in a battle for equal educational rights, and the struggle must now be transferred to the virtual society. We cannot continue to rest. . . because women now achieve comparable results to men in print-based systems and assessments.

> (Spender, 1995: 210)

For e-moderators, it is important to be sensitive to any individual or group that appears to be disadvantaged or not participating online. While it is difficult to police harassment and inappropriate behaviour on public listservers and the like, these cannot be allowed in any kind of educational environment. Harassment of any kind must be stopped immediately online, as it is on campuses and in corporate environments, to ensure equality of learning opportunity for all. In particular, e-moderators should regularly consider the tone of their messages and their online behaviour (and be open to monitoring from their peers), to ensure that no exploitation of their more powerful position occurs, even inadvertently.

E-moderators and lurkers

In the exit questionnaire from the e-moderator training described in Chapter 4, I ask the trainees their level of engagement with the training programme and their maintenance of interest throughout. This question is intended to elicit a crude notion of whether trainees have, by the end of the five-stage programme, become active users and whether the software has facilitated this. However, the question is typically answered in a more sophisticated and expansive way than I originally expected. Although over three-quarters of the trainees report 'active participation' online, half also point out the value of 'passive' participation, ie browsing, 'listening' or lurking. Late starters in the programme are more likely to report 'passive' engagement than early starters (who perhaps had more opportunities to complete the online activities). This suggests that timing (and considerable amounts of time) to get used to communicating online, are very important.

The OUBS participation figures show a very wide range of response to CMC, from willingness to spend huge amounts of time and mental energy to a need to be online but to 'browse' before actively contributing. We have therefore re-labelled 'lurking' as 'browsing' in an attempt to recognize this need in some individuals and to remove the negative connotations. If, however, the majority of members of a conference are browsing, it is time for a rethink and redesign of the purpose and activities of the conference. There is no doubt that the more active participants become upset with browsers, however. Managing the interface between contributing and browsing is a key e-moderating task.

A face-to-face facilitator is often able to ascertain from body language why a learner is listening rather than contributing. The listeners form the audience and they may be nodding agreement, applauding or sleeping! The e-moderator cannot look at the audience and determine its reaction in the same way. Indeed, some browsers visit but leave no trace of their presence other than in the message history. Try and establish why they are browsing, if necessary contacting them by e-mail or telephone.

Are lurkers learning? It looks as though many are, and some are unabashed about this:

> As a confirmed lurker, I have found the conferences stimulating and broadening. It is seldom possible to access views from such a wide range of backgrounds. There are individual contributors whom I will always seek out in particular where I have found their solutions to questions of benefit. NH

From the OUBS conferences, we noticed three main types (Dence, 1996):

1. The freeloader

> It has come to my attention that we have a large number of lurkers and freeloaders in this conference (don't take offence – just my way with words). I am not saying that a lurker is a bad person but I am saying that a lurker is using my contribution and giving me nothing in return. And that makes me feel some grievance. My experience of such things is that *what you get out* is in proportion to *what you put in*. So feel free to contribute!! PN

2. The sponge

> In fact, in lurking in this particular area, I am getting good tuition both in the use of the medium and in the vocabulary (jargon, if you like) of an area of knowledge that is new to me and into which I would hesitate to insert a contribution. AB

3. Lurkers with skills or access problems

> I'm lost. Please help me. I just can't remember how to post a reply to the right conference that will get me help. I'm in a loop. I'm really upset about the combative tone of the active people in the course conferences – I'm really not here as a thief you know! GK

Learners generally browse before they are ready to contribute – and, as you have seen from the model in Chapter 2, this happens in different ways and at different paces. Sometimes a participant would have posted a message but does not because what the participant wanted to contribute has already been said by another member of the conference (Rossman, 1999). Often they contribute on a topic or at a level with which they feel comfortable, perhaps in a different conference. However, most participants are put off by a conference that is constantly domin-ated by one or two individuals (including sometimes the e-moderator!). The names of such over-keen individuals get spotted and other participants fall away. E-moderators need to watch carefully for this happening, as groups often find dominant individuals more difficult to deal with online than they might face-to-face. The solution is to encourage dominant individuals into e-mail or to set up conferences of their own and create increased structure in your learning conferences.

OU Master's course case study

David Hawkridge's example of students' response demonstrates the wide variety of responses and the patterns of communications that develop between widely dispersed participants. David Hawkridge, an e-moderator, writes:

> From February to October each year I tutor 10–20 students who are taking a 600-hour Open University (OU) course called Foundations of Open and Distance Education, offered by the Institute of Educa-tional Technology (http://www-iet.open.ac.uk). My students live in many countries besides the United Kingdom. They receive print, video, audio and CD ROM course materials, but must also have access to e-mail and the Web. On average, I'm in e-mail contact with each student about once a week. They also send me six assignments via the Web site: I mark them on screen and add comments before returning them electronically, usually two or three days after receiving them. En route, the marks are recorded automatically at the OU, and the marked assignment may be copied for quality control purposes.
>
> The password-protected Web site is essential to the course. It provides a welcome page, online text resources, an assignment sub-mission page and entry to the electronic database of the OU's Inter-national Centre for Distance Learning and to a site for alumni. From our welcome page, students and tutors move directly into a bulletin board system (BBS) divided into a plenary discussion area for all and areas for each tutor group. This is where I e-moderate conferences in my own group and help with those in the plenary area.
>
> I've learned a lot over the last three years about how students, most of them new to all this, respond in the different conferences. In the plenary area, there's a noticeboard, an area for discussing course

themes and issues, a café and 'ask the experts'. Students read the noticeboard but, no surprise, seldom reply to any of the messages there unless there's a panic about something. By contrast, the course themes and issues generate discussion, often based on activities written into the materials. Here are some threads (conversations) for Activity 2.2, which is about Donald Schön's writings on reflective practitioners. The last two messages are about how to save Web pages onto your own computer, because one student wanted to do that. The e-moderator (me, David) chimed in four times. Notice that no women joined in this time.

no 82 Activity 2.2 17 Feb 99, Neville-g
no 89 Reflections on Schön and Eraut 18 Feb 99, David
no 95 Reflections on Activity 2.2 18 Feb 99, Stephen-m
no 100 It works for me 18 Feb 99, Neville-g
no 126 Ahhhhhhh 21 Feb 99, Christopher-h
no 127 Practising in a 2nd generation institute 21 Feb 99, Christopher-h
no 136 Reflection-for-action 22 Feb 99, David
no 143 Reflection on reflection 22 Feb 99, James-c
no 172 Group therapy 25 Feb 99, Christopher-h
no 173 Shooting students 26 Feb 99, David
no 237 Over egging the pudding 25 Mar 99, Neville-g
no 242 Web grabbing 26 Mar 99, Christopher-h
no 243 Web Grabber 29 Mar 99, David

In the café everybody introduces themselves – some only in late March – and each message usually gets at least one cheery rejoinder, from a student or a tutor. By mid-1999, with about 40 students on the course, the café had well over 200 messages. Students start threads spontaneously, puzzling about course content and technical problems as well as exchange social pleasantries. Some threads end after a couple of messages, others are much longer.

'Ask the experts' gives students a chance to put questions to a few well-known experts who agree to join the BBS. For a week in May this year, students were in touch with the author of the study guide they were reading at the time. She responded to their detailed questions. I didn't have to moderate that conference at all, merely start it.

Just as in conferencing systems elsewhere, most messages come from about a third of the students, with another third fairly active and the rest very seldom writing anything after the first introductions. As e-moderator, I don't try to stimulate specific students to contribute, although I can see from the system statistics how many times each student has visited the BBS. Lurking abounds, of course, though students rightly object to the term and prefer 'browsing'. Students (and tutors) can read any message anywhere in the BBS for this course.

With my own group, two kinds of conferences develop each year. One, like the course themes and issues in the plenary area, is based on the course content. The other is a series of workshops, one for each assignment. Over the three years, block conferences have generated useful threads, some of them really long. I regard myself as an equal participant in these threads, although I suppose it's true that the students expect me to be more knowledgeable than they are. Last year, quite a lot of discussion occurred in this one. So far this year, there's been only a handful of messages.

Assignment workshops are usually extremely active, but that's because there's a percentage (usually 20) of marks allocated for appropriate use in assignments of quotes from the threads. Not all tutors agree that this is a good idea, though it does stimulate the conferencing. The problem lies in devising sound criteria for allocating the 20 per cent.

I take the initiative in the workshops by posting a longish message containing hints about how to approach the assignment, which is always an essay of 2,000 or 4,000 words. Students comment on what I've said, and as moderator I don't usually enter the thread much, leaving it to them to discuss the assignment with each other. I can intervene, of course, if somebody raises a knotty problem or misunderstands something in the course materials. I do read all the messages. Here are the threads for the second assignment (TMA02), spread over 20 days. This time the women joined in, and so did I:

no 59 TMA Workshop for TMA02 04 Mar 99, David
no 60 reply to TMA02 04 Mar 99, Hilary-g
no 61 Activity 4.1 – Closed?? 05 Mar 99, Christopher-h
no 62 Technology and openness 08 Mar 99, Stephen-m
no 63 Reply 08 Mar 99, Melanie-j
no 76 Hi from Big Brother! 13 Mar 99, Nigel
no 64 Technologies 08 Mar 99, Hilary-g
no 85 Passing control to students 15 Mar 99, Beverley-p
no 86 Sorry for the intrusion! 15 Mar 99, Beverley-p
no 102 No apology needed, Beverley 20 Mar 99, David
no 65 Independent learning? 08 Mar 99, Hilary-g
no 66 Right on, Hilary and everyone else! 09 Mar 99, David
no 67 Beautifully refreshing Activity 4.8 09 Mar 99, Christopher-h
no 68 Johnson 1990 P80 S4 B1 10 Mar 99, Neville-g
no 69 Johnson again 10 Mar 99, Neville-g
no 71 The written word 10 Mar 99, Stephen-m
no 77 Selling OL 13 Mar 99, David
no 80 OL vs. DE 15 Mar 99, Neville-g
no 81 To continue the argument 15 Mar 99, Melanie-j
no 70 Activity 4.1 10 Mar 99, Neville-g

no 73 Johnson's Second Point 11 Mar 99, Melanie-j
no 75 Johnson!! 13 Mar 99, David
no 78 More Activity 4.8 14 Mar 99, Christopher-h
no 79 TMA02: straight to the point 14 Mar 99, Bustami-k
no 90 To continue the discussion 16 Mar 99, Melanie-j
no 91 Error in TMA02: straight to the point. 16 Mar 99, Bustami-k
no 94 Brownie Point Earner 17 Mar 99, Neville-g
no 97 Help 17 Mar 99, Neville-g
no 98 Help -2 17 Mar 99, Neville-g
no 99 Meaning? 19 Mar 99, David
no 108 Commenting on comments 23 Mar 99, Neville-g
no 109 Chunking the messages 24 Mar 99, David
no 111 HTML 3/26/99, Christopher-h
no 92 Defining learners' needs – who and how? 17 Mar 99, Bustami-k
no 95 Assistance 17 Mar 99, Neville-g
no 96 Assistance 2nd try 17 Mar 99, Neville-g
no 93 Who meets the needs? 17 Mar 99, Melanie-j
no 100 Defining our terms 19 Mar 99, Stephen-m
no 101 Learners' sacrifices 19 Mar 99, Bustami-k
no 103 Society 21-Mar-99, Christopher-h
no 104 The Rolling Stones 21 Mar 99, Christopher-h
no 110 On the ball, Nora! 24 Mar 99, David

It's amazing, but I've never seen a real case of flaming anywhere in our BBS. The nearest to it was one year when two students, one Greek, the other British, were discussing at length the philosophical foundations of truth. One finally accused the other, hotly, of being unprincipled, even amoral. The other just laughed (yes, online) and said he had better get on with his assignment! I wish I could quote the messages to you, but of course the copyright in them rests with the students concerned. They both finished the course with good marks, though I did notice that the first one changed from being a very active contributor to a browser.

E-moderating does take time, and I don't think we know enough yet about how to do it both well and quickly. I watch my fellow tutors by reading their group conferences from time to time: their style is not the same as mine, but they seem to do a good job. One responds at length and in detail, but less often than I do. One has a great sense of humour. One is incredibly laid back and seems to be appreciated by many of his students. I'll keep an eye on their e-moderating and pick up some tips.

Participant induction

Steeples and her colleagues suggest that a face-to-face meeting is appropriate for induction, especially for small groups, because of the bonding that occurs and

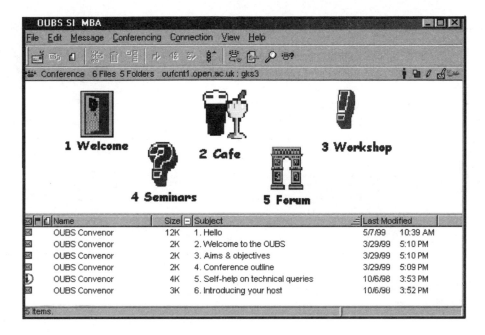

Figure 5.1   *Desktop screen of student induction in OUBS*

because early problems can be ironed out on the spot (Steeples, Vincent and Chapman, 1997). Such a meeting is not always feasible, however, or may be simply too expensive, as it is for the Open University's Business School (see Chapter 4). All the School's MBA students are offered an online induction programme immediately prior to or at the start of their courses. Software is mailed to them when they register (Salmon, 1998b). The programme uses the five-stage model discussed in Chapter 2 and is based on the experience gained in our online e-moderator training programmes.

We found in the OUBS that it is possible to use many of the messages from e-moderator training for the student induction. Issues such as communication styles are included, as well as key software skills. At levels four and five, conferences are offered to enable the students to use CMC to prepare them for study. At level four, the emphasis is on setting and sharing personal objectives and study skills and at level five discussing key management topics.

The induction conferences remain available to students in a non-interactive form during the year. They are visited or revisited by other students and as a reminder by some of those who have already taken part.

Following the first online induction conferences for OU MBA students, informal feedback from the students' conferences was positive and contributed to the largest ever use of CMC in the OUBS in 1997. Participation rates and purposefulness have gradually built up since then. See Gray and Salmon (1999) for responses in a large-scale course.

Students with little experience of technological applications before a course begins may find it all but impossible to undertake the course itself as well as getting to grips with problems of the technology. They face many of the same issues that trainee e-moderators face, for example, 'red flag' overload (in FirstClass unread messages are shown with a red flag). With up to 100 students over a short period of time in each conference, e-moderating may be needed almost daily.

Exit questionnaires and follow-up e-mails collected student feedback after their induction into the world of FirstClass CMC in the OU Business School. On the whole, student responses to online induction are very positive:

> Brilliant... EVC
>
> ... an excellent tool. DF
>
> I think it will make all the difference. EV
>
> Conferencing is of great help to students be they in an English city or miles away from anywhere somewhere else in the world. When you hit a low there is always someone there to pick you up and dust you off. You can bounce ideas off people. It is easy dip into a conference for a few minutes each day or week. I have never been involved in face-to-face self-study groups but these must take a lot more organizing and time for the event itself. PS
>
> It gave me the initial confidence boost I think most people require when entering the unknown. DG

Others were convinced during the induction and went on to become active course conference participants:

> Despite my limited participation due to time constraint, I found that ideas and issues raised developed fast and feedback is almost immediate. Online discussions have a life and a genre of their own! The outcome of such conferences is interesting and useful. NM

The most commonly expressed doubts and concerns about CMC for learning are about time (set against the rest of the course's demands) and how to strike a balance between studying, working and domestic life.

> It is useful but gets clogged with messages that don't add *value for me*. I wasted a lot of time on it initially and felt inadequate when I couldn't keep up with all of the new messages, but I do find I get some useful info. I tend to set a time limit and stick to it. RA

And finally an e-moderator's advice to participants:

> Don't assume that those people already on the system are experts – some
> may well be only one step ahead of you! Ask the obvious questions – (others
> may have the same problem and be grateful to you). RB

I hope this chapter has convinced you of the importance for all e-moderators to
understand (rather than 'see') the variety of issues and needs that each participant
will bring to his or her online conference. Induction for all is important, at least
for the foreseeable future.

The following Resources for practitioners provide summaries and some
practical ideas:

Chapter 6

E-moderating: the key to the future of online teaching and learning

No book of this kind, written during the infancy of online teaching, can be complete without an attempt to plan for what is on the horizon. Everyone knows it's hazardous to predict the future as it's easy for the writer to look wrong-footed within a few years (or even months when we're talking about networked technologies!). However, I think we can be sure that more learners will soon receive all or part of their education or training online. Perhaps only small percentages of the content of some courses will be delivered through electronic means, but many of those institutions that stick firmly to face-to-face or print-based teaching systems are unlikely to be in the field for much longer. Online education might eventually become standard with just a few élite face-to-face campus universities and training schools remaining.

I hope in this chapter to raise your awareness of the need for imaginative e-moderation to embrace a range of new directions. The most successful educators of the future will not be those who keep up with the race to put content on the Web or on CD ROMs, but those who can predict and act on the less obvious, weaker signals coming from the environment, and then work out how to enable productive, happy, e-moderating for learning (Salmon, 2000). I consider here what those opportunities might be. I believe that even a rough and ready chart is better than no map at all. I highlight a few key areas that will have an impact on the work of e-moderators: the changing educational environment, the nature of future CMC participants and communities and the impact of online teaching and learning on assessment. I risk a view of the up-and-coming technologies and throw out a challenge to those responsible for providing us with the tools of our trade – the CMC software creators and manufacturers. Each area has a developing body of literature for you to explore. I hope I shall stimulate you to create your own map of the future for e-moderating in your own context.

The changing education environment

One question we must ask, to which there is no simple answer at present, is whether it is worthwhile to invest in e-moderating and everything that surrounds it. The sceptics are rife and, quite naturally and properly, some teachers and academics question CMC's value for learning. Furthermore, the economics of online learning are still to be established along with stakeholder and budgeting models. The stakes and the costs of innovation are high. Will the notion of ownership of information be gradually displaced by the far greater need to explore, explain, and support positions through online argument and evidence? There will be legal implications in such a shift. There are many debates still to come about intellectual property rights and online privacy and security (Agre and Rotenberg, 1997). Changing the roles of academics and teachers challenges established patterns and creates concern, horror even, in those who believe we risk quality ('dumbing down') in learning provision. Meanwhile, I sense an increasing interest in the key issue of online communication and interaction between people for high quality learning and the huge added value and import- ance of good e-moderation. Some of the most forward-looking practitioners are already addressing this challenge directly. Jean-Louis Michelet, a founding execu- tive of the International Cyber University of Singapore (http://www.icus.net) suggests that the key success factor in online learning will be in the creation of beneficial human interaction through e-moderators (he calls them e-coaches). Maybe the quality of online learning will be judged as impaired or enhanced by e-moderators' interventions and support? Perhaps that is how we make online learning pay dividends and enhance quality?

Besides CMC, there are other major changes occurring in the world of online teaching and learning. These include complex associations between technology and network providers, publishers and educational institutions. New types of organizations are being set up: some are new to education and others build on allies with 'brand' names. At the time of writing, the news has just broken of a merger between Time Warner and AOL to create a fully integrated media and communications company. Other such merger proposals are likely to follow suit, with as yet unknown implications for the changing world of education.

At the same time, learners' awareness of their choices as customers is growing. Although there is concern from students and sponsors about the quality of many new courses, programmes and qualifications, word will quickly 'get around' in our fast networked world about which educational provider looks after its online students and makes available a great learning experience. Potential new markets for online learning are identified and created as educational providers explore competitive advantages, niche or global markets and specialist expertise. As Mary Beth Susman says:

> Where once students revolved around their higher education institution, going from department to department, office to office, class to class to gather their services, telecommunications provides the ability to have institutions revolve around their students... Students log in at any time of day from any location. (Susman, 1999: 24)

As this new virtual educational marketplace develops, demand for more e-moderators will rise, possibly exponentially, to provide the meaning and the human touch. In parallel, there will be a movement away from notions of presenting online 'content' and 'instruction', towards greater construction of knowledge through CMC.

The pace of 'unbundling' the various components of teaching and learning will speed up, I believe, leaving e-moderating as a discrete function in online learning. Perhaps online teaching in universities will be professionalized and specialized, instead of the role being embedded in those of scholar and researcher as at present. The most celebrated teachers in future may not be those with high profile publications but those best able to mediate knowledge for CMC participants. Many e-moderators will work part-time, from home with other full-time jobs as well as their e-moderating duties, thus having a strong link into their non-educational worlds.

Changing learners and learning to change

The learners of the near future will be what Greg Dyke, current Director-General of the BBC, calls the 'playstation generation'. They will be accustomed to highly immediate, interactive, visual electronic resources. They will want learning that is: 'Just in time, just for me, just a keystroke, just for now' (Spender, 1999).

In future, even more than in the past, the kind of businesses and organizations that develop, and how people earn and spend, will be intrinsically bound up with how and what people learn. The pressure on educational institutions to respond to rapidly evolving business environments will build up (DiPaolo, 1999). Career switches will be frequent and training and education a constant and life-long requirement. Distinctions between work and learning will blur. Cosmopolitan communities will create openness about race and belief, with less hierarchy and with members who desire to learn from widely scattered and less formal sources. Long-living, long-working, independent learners will be mobile and pragmatic. They will become comfortable and skilful in choosing from a vast electronic array of opportunities. The idea of a requirement for qualifications to enter courses will seem to be quaint (Spender, 1999). As students and informal learners become more discerning, they may start to demand control not only over when and where they learn, but also over the content (Young and Marks-Maran, 1999).

Skills needed for work and learning will embrace self-direction together with a willingness to support others, the ability to work in multi-skilled teams (which are likely to operate without regular meetings), to co-operate rather than compete, to handle information (rather than know everything) and to become critical thinkers (Salmon, 1999b). Regy Loknes, Senior Learning and Development Adviser for Shell, explains that a change of learning mindset is needed. He wants future recruits to be able to 'know how they learn, know what they need to learn and be open and receptive to learning from others without negative responses and criticisms' (Loknes, 2000).

CMC's characteristics are those of openness and participation but achieving learning outcomes through CMC works best within structured programmes and with careful and frequent e-moderation. Most professional education and training to date has focused on discrete courses. In the OUBS and most of the case studies in this book, the teaching processes were quite strictly scheduled. They began at a certain time, with learning and assessment methodologies built in, and they finished with tests or examinations. Within the programmes, along the way, participants experienced small successes, which they deemed to be very important. Will future education include such discrete structured courses? As individuals become more and more networked, they demand very much smaller 'chunks' of relevant learning, backed up by connections and explorative opportunities with like-minded others. The assessment of knowledge and competence then becomes an issue as I indicate later in this chapter. Charles Jennings offers us a radical view of the professional learner of the future:

> There is a distinct trend away from 'courses' towards performance support models in professional development. I think that CMC environments will be important in this new 'knowledge-driven' world. However, these CMC environments will overwhelmingly be used for (sometimes structured) performance support rather than as conduits for formal 'courses'. The conference e-moderator will transmogrify into the online mentor and support agent. . . the online conference will evolve into a self-structuring searchable knowledge-base, and learning peers will become fused into a 'permanently on' digital world. We won't just access this through our computers, but through a wealth of digital devices including our telephones, our wristwatches, our Personal Digital Assistant (PDA), and even our house-hold appliances.
>
> (Jennings, 1999)

But whatever happens to course and programme structures, we can be sure that the human factor – the role of the e-moderator – will be critical in the accepta-bility and success of online learning communities. Who otherwise will support newcomers to a body of knowledge or practice? Newcomers might otherwise treat, with equal deference, bizarre as well as sane contributions and the tenden-tious in addition to well-evidenced pieces of information.

Interaction for online knowledge construction gets to the heart of what most CMC participants consider important. They feel intuitively that knowledge is not just about data or information but is much richer, broader and linked with personal experience in complex ways. In a world where knowledge is the key resource for the future, a primary ingredient of everything 'we do, we make, buy and sell' (Stewart, 1997), the issue of how it can be surfaced and articulated for learning will become even more important. Links between learning and knowledge management systems will be made more explicit. I anticipate that understandings of the social origin of psychological processes (Vygotsky, 1978) and how these occur in the online environment will grow through research. The role of the university will change from 'ivory tower' to 'market place', from sole provider of knowledge to synergizer of multiple sources (Haddad, 2000). Professor Tim O'Shea, Master of Birkbeck College, University of London, suggests that research-rich institutions will be those that grow, thrive and have the most to offer to the networked world of online learning. E-moderators will enable knowledge sharing, and, wherever possible and appropriate, knowledge generation.

Online learning communities and associations will not be based on a sense of place but of purpose or profession and more emphasis will be placed on building trust, resolving conflict and solving problems. As Dr Andy DiPaolo of Stanford Center for Professional Development says:

> E-moderation for creating a sense of a learning community is the key to success! . . . we should help learners to truly feel part of their course, to feel special and to experience a unique and integrated world around the topic under study. They can join a discussion group with active professionals from the field, they can undertake electronic field trips, and they can engage in activities orchestrated by a skilled e-moderator which will make the experience of learning both richer and more relevant to the world of work.

> (DiPaolo, 2000)

Individuals will develop skills in socializing in many different ways simultaneously and be able to adopt appropriate roles online. Cross-cultural awareness stimulates recognition of the need to understand cognitive processes better, to become more receptive and more accepting of differing intellectual styles and modes of thought and to reduce the arrogance sometimes associated with traditional thinking. Groups from very different understandings, backgrounds, cultures and 'voices' (Latchem and Lockwood, 1998) will learn together and gain access to competing or contradictory ideas. A major role for e-moderators will be to enable surfacing, understandings and collaboration across cultures.

Globally, 700 million people use English, with half of these with English as their second language. Significantly for CMC, English has become the main language of the Internet. In future, we will need to understand better the impact of using English online. Does the use of English imply acceptance of certain cultural traditions? In the United Kingdom, for instance, the model of teaching and learning is based on acceptance of a certain level of independence. Other cultures' teaching traditions may give the impression that the 'teacher is king', thus posing a challenge to e-moderators aiming for democratic and collaborative approaches.

As the use of media other than onscreen text becomes commoner, will the models change again? The implications for education as a whole could be profound. In the more distant future, dramatic changes will doubtless occur across a range of economic functions, new concepts of space and time will be created, novel forms of communities will be established and ultimately human thinking will change. The power of CMC for learning could mould, shape and construct changes rather than merely be responsive to them. The distances involved in like-minded groups wishing to interact may finally defeat the notion of 'attending' for learning.

CMC and assessment processes

For the foreseeable future, most participants will want to achieve qualifications, accreditation or awards, so assessment in some form or other will be necessary. Indeed, many course designers find that assessment is the engine that drives and motivates students (Brown, Bull and Race, 1999). Most learners crave teachers' responses to their coursework and their examinations. Learners see the quality and quantity of feedback on their work as an important part of their relationships with their professors and educational provider.

As you have seen throughout this book, the use of e-moderated CMC for learning directly addresses the broadening acceptance and understanding of learning as a socially mediated and constructed process (Billett, 1996) and of knowledge as personal and not 'fixed' (Hendry, 1996). However, many assessment procedures are still based on the transmission model of information. This means that unless issues of evaluation and assessment are tackled as the use of CMC for learning increases the gap between how students learn and how they are assessed may widen. Some students already comment on the irony of spending most of their learning time communicating through their computer, but taking their examination in a formal setting with only a pen and paper for company. As e-moderators become more comfortable with their online teaching roles, I think they will start to look closely at online assessment and evaluation, and will not wish their time and their students' time to be constrained by old assessment methods. Highly networked organizations such as professional associations are already waking up to the huge potential of 'any time, any place' assessment.

CMC offers more opportunities for students to write for themselves to benefit their own learning and also for each other (rather than 'writing for the tutor'). Through CMC, students can make their writing easily available for review and assessment. As a start, suggest to CMC participants that they should use conference messages in their assignments and that they will be given credit for their ability to use and integrate messages in their work. You might like to try a peer review process of students' written work, even if their essays, assignments or exercises are afterwards handed in for marking by a teacher/assessor. If you try such a process, ensure that the criteria for judgements are made explicit from the start and based on learning outcomes.

As with CMC software, networked and multimedia technology offers new possibilities for online assessment. The OU and a number of other universities, such as the Dutch OU and Monash in Melbourne, have introduced opportunities for students to submit their assignments electronically and for tutors to mark, comment and return them online. However, this is only the first step in what might become a revolution in assessment processes. More universities will innovate in online assessment, usually based on campus networks using commercial software. Several pioneers are already addressing important concerns (O'Reilly and Morgan, 1999). These include issues of access and security, plagiarism and cheating (is this work really my student's?), the time and costs of setting up (efficiency gains), dealing with bias, fairness and anxiety, and test design and implementation of systems (Brown, Bull and Race, 1999). Experiments in assessment for online and open learning environments are starting (see, for example, Cann and Pawley, 1999) and student reactions so far are highly positive. It is likely that students, as customers, will drive this sensitive but important area further towards online provision in the future. A corollary will be the need for the valid assessment of the performance of large numbers of learners at low cost.

Developing, combining and converging technologies

Any list of 'new technologies' I might compile will risk becoming obsolete by the time you read this, but it is certain that networked technologies will be further developed and combined in the near future, especially those that can be delivered to individual computer desktops. CMC will continue to become more widely available and accessible.

Currently, the 'richness' of the Web depends largely on its volume and the multimedia presentation of information. However, I believe the next steps are towards greater interaction – and interaction is fundamental to learning, so long as it is appropriately e-moderated and embedded in the overall learning methods. CMC technologies and the mix of media will become more sophisticated and integrated. The debate about keeping costs down (typically through low bandwidth using text) and increasing functionality (typically through high bandwidth, for multimedia) of networked technologies is likely to continue for a while. Systems will become faster, working with greater functionality. New forms of digital libraries will emerge and with them new roles for e-librarians keen to work with e-moderators. The opportunities for teaching and learning with each new development will need exploring early and rapidly lest the technology races ahead of our understanding of the usefulness of each application. The need will always be there for e-moderators to offer pathways and routes, and to make sense of online experiences by seeing the threads and connections, perhaps with better CMC software support.

The configuration of the personal computer, keyboard and monitor has changed little since the early 1980s. The users still primarily interact with their keyboards, which disadvantages those with few keyboarding skills. Three key technological changes that will impact on e-moderation are occurring as I write this book. The first is voice recognition software; the second synchronous voice conferencing and the third more mobile, portable connectivity. As discussed in Chapter 5, offering various ways of accessing online conferencing widens access and offers more options to e-moderators.

Voice or speech recognition software has been primitive and inaccurate for most users until recently but low-priced portable voice recognition software will soon become more available. The reliability of the software is improving along with a reduction in the computer processing power required. Voice recognition will soon become a viable option for most computer users (Semaan, 2000). Voice recognition over the telephone will provide automated information provision. Within a conference, a participant will be able to 'say' a contribution.

The use of synchronous conferencing through the Internet offers participants the feeling of immediate contact, motivation and some fun, which is especially valuable if they are studying largely alone and at a distance, or where there's a need for them to experience a wide range of learning opportunities. Synchronous Internet audio conferencing has been used productively by the OU on foreign language programmes, where it offers benefits to distance learners to develop, helps them to develop oral and aural skills in the target language and to converse spontaneously (Rodine, Kotter and Shield, 1999).

Following a number of research and development projects, OU MBA students are using Internet audio-based synchronous conferencing. They use a software tool called Lyceum conceived and prototyped at the OU's Knowledge Media Institute (KMI) and implemented by a team at the OU's Centre for Educational Software. Lyceum supports Internet audio, dynamic onscreen whiteboard, concept mapper, and image grabber. Voice quality is nearly as good as telephony. See Scott and Eisenstadt (1998) and http://kmi.open.ac.uk/knowledgeweb for overview of Lyceum and examples of synchronous technologies.

Professor Paul Quintas of the Open University Business School writes about the experience on an MBA course using Lyceum:

> We rolled out a synchronous audio conferencing tool to nearly 1000 MBA students on *B823 Managing Knowledge* course. Participants are located globally – we have students in Australia, Asia and South Africa as well as throughout Europe. The onscreen tools provide many advantages over telephone conferencing such as participants being able to see who is talking, or who is waiting to speak. Learning teams can jointly develop on-screen shared diagrams or concept maps, and discuss these in real time. Lyceum supports small group structured activities (three or four students), tutorials (e-moderator plus up to 12 students) plus a burgeoning number of informal uses, eg groups of students running their own self-help groups on a drop-in basis. During online tutorials e-moderators can control the screen display of all the students' personal computers and talk through presentation slides. A great deal of work has gone into the design and e-moderation of the online tutorials, building on the experience of good face to face facilitators. Although systematic evaluation is not yet complete, from my experience

so far I think that synchronous conferencing can support real learning. Synchronous conferencing has huge potential for distance learning because it provides the advantages of real-time discussions and group interactions without the need for specialized telecommunications channels or for participants to co-locate.

On another front, the pace of technological change in the huge and competitive market for mobile Internet connectivity is rapidly accelerating. Phone numbers will in future identify an individual rather than a device or geographical location and phone numbers may last for the life of an individual person. Public telephone networks, originally created for voice transmission, will transform to carry data (text, sound and video), mostly based on Internet technologies. Low orbit wireless satellite access to all corners of the world, together with falling prices for computer and communications technologies, will give much wider access and networking on a truly global scale. In countries with poor fixed-line telephone systems, mobile connectivity through cellular systems will provide access to many more people who will 'leap-frog' over others, technologically, by missing out interim stages. How interesting and valuable it will be to have such wide perspectives made available in our online conferencing! Mobile phones will perform much wider functions than voice calls. Eventually, we will be wearing, rather than carrying, our personal computers. They will receive and transmit video images, text messages and Internet information. Audio and video conferencing through the Web will become common. Perhaps digital interactive TV may finally prove to be the 'killer' educational application of the future, sweeping aside other technology due to its very wide availability?

The challenge for software developers

I believe that the truly great CMC software, driven by a full understanding of e-moderation, has yet to be developed. The key challenges for software developers come from course team members, students, e-moderators, corporate learning departments and designers, who all want much cheaper, easier access to CMC, from anywhere, without any online security compromise and with more e-moderating tools embedded in the software! Can CMC software developers ensure that we will spend less time mastering the software, so that we can have more time to e-moderate, collaborate and learn? Can they reduce the need for special hardware or high bandwidth for remote users? Can they offer effective ways of working offline but with easy connectivity?

There are other challenges for the software developers. Practitioners and researchers will be satisfied when they can easily:

- observe what is happening online without interfering in the variety of events and conferences;
- demonstrate, to potential students and clients, the power and complexity of what is occurring online without having to give full access;

- create, structure, maintain and manage online conferences, eg to group and regroup individuals online without technical support;
- enhance the essentially text-based conferencing environment in an increasingly visual online world;
- use hypertext links so that they can embed documents and other applications into the conference structures and work on shared attachments in conferences;
- enhance the use of metaphors online and provide interesting and purposeful learning environments onscreen through a wide range of icons and visual techniques (easily found and used and driven by the e-moderators not the technicians).

For CMC to fulfil its true potential for knowledge construction there will be ways of making use of previous online discussion. Much of the value of CMC for learning is in the taking part and the constructing of knowledge through the experience of working online. However, if online discussions are searchable or captured in an easily assimilated way, later participants start from a slightly different and potentially more information-rich and knowledgeable place than previous cohorts did. Improvements will be made in CMC software for the stages of collaborative learning and critical thinking. Software will be designed that goes beyond the rudimentary 'threading' and linking structures that are currently provided in proprietary software. The software tools will need to support more complex reading, contributing and organizing of ideas, and ways of building these into shared and constructed knowledge bases. More creative and free-flowing thinking and conferencing could then be supported. E-moderators will then have a new role – providing selection and codification of the knowledge generated by conferencing in order to articulate and make it available to new groups. Perhaps a new generation of CMC software can be developed that has its roots in knowledge management (rather than messaging systems or databases) that will truly close the gap between managing knowledge and online learning?

Conclusions

There is a developing paradox. Networking is becoming ever wider through CMC and is gradually becoming global. However, what an individual wants or needs from the potential of wide networking is very individual and focused. Resolving this paradox remains one of the key opportunities for education for the foreseeable future. Almost every individual who comes into contact with CMC recognizes its potential for learning and the complex interplay between the technology, the acquiring of software skills and their use as teaching and learning tools. Even those who are reluctant or perhaps fearful acknowledge this. However, in each case, the desire for an easy to use and purposeful environment is very strong. From this I predict that as the hardware becomes faster, the software easier to use and more sophisticated, and the entry skills of the users better honed, so access to and motivation towards using networked technologies for learning will increase.

Increasing access and speed will not replace the need for induction into the use of CMC, however, nor for the creation of productive online learning environments, nor for ever-increasing skills and sophistication in e-moderating techniques.

Learning and teaching institutions adapt to changing circumstances and new technologies and they will do so again. The challenge of developing new kinds of online teaching, learning and research communities, while remaining true to an educational or training mission, will be at the forefront of the implementation of information and communication technologies in the early 21st century. Perhaps, in time, the great teachers and educators of the Web will have their names placed alongside those of Sid Meier, developer of the game Civilisation, and Miyamoto, developer of Mario, who are already seen as visionaries and artists?

The ripples created by networked technologies are now flowing over businesses throughout the world, with an impact on learning provision. The needs and expectations of individuals and their employees for education and training of all kinds are changing accordingly. Competition, notions of quality and relevance of learning are entering a new era. The paradoxes of increasingly global business with very individualized approaches to learning, will challenge the heart of well-loved and rehearsed distance learning teaching and learning methods. CMC has a unique and valuable place in the debates and the emerging practices, with the focus on the role of e-moderating for successful learning.

Perhaps from these small beginnings we can build a new body of knowledge and practice for online teaching and learning that will transfer again and again as new and even more connected technologies become available. I believe that the need for developed and skilful e-moderators will not disappear, regardless of how sophisticated and fast moving the technological tools become.

More and more people will have access to CMC. CMC participants contribute and experience the learning. E-moderators add the real value! I think that the most successful teaching and learning organizations and associations will be those that understand, recruit, train, support and give free creative rein to their e-moderators, while addressing the natural fears of loss of power and quality from traditional university faculty members. E-moderating will become a key competitive advantage. So there's a risky prediction for you! Perhaps even one we can measure!

E-moderators can take control, make it good, make it real and make it worthwhile. I hope the five-stage model and other ideas in this book will give you inspiration. Let's keep in touch and e-moderate the future, together.

To explore further the ideas in this chapter, look at the following Resources for practitioners:

Part 2: RESOURCES FOR PRACTITIONERS

The following provide a variety of resources for you to try out with your students and e-moderators. All are research based and have their roots in practice, commonly in the OU or OUBS or sometimes in my consultancy practice. None are intended to be definitive, but they provide you with checklists to make your own or to use as the basis of resources for online or offline workshops and discussions.

Resources for practitioners 1

Choosing a software system for CMC

We all know there is plenty of hype about new technology. Software systems for CMC suffer from it as much as any. Yet choosing software for CMC requires a long, cool appraisal, preferably with the help of other people who will be using it too. There is no ideal CMC system that suits everyone, so choices lie ahead.

First, if you are clear about your own educational or training agenda, you should aim to select CMC software that more or less fits that agenda. Some suppliers try to sell software based on little more than a rudimentary rote training model. Others have software that makes possible highly interactive collaborative group work, with knowledge construction.

Second, you may wish to outsource CMC systems and/or service support rather than buying or setting up your own. It may be a good idea to outsource whilst you try out some systems and processes.

Third, it should pay to get a debate going in your own department and others that may have an interest in the final decision. Raise questions like these about the system that you want:

1. What is the underlying model or concept of teaching and learning and how does it fit with your own ideas? For example, does it assume a lecturer or trainer as the primary source of knowledge? Does it assume a primary role for testing rather than teaching?
2. Are there internal political reasons, or external customer/supplier reasons, why you are likely to have to choose one software system over another anyway?
3. Are you promised features in the next version that you think are important now? If so, look for other systems that already have these.

4.   Can the system be used on a large enough scale, with many users online at once (ask other large users and think about peak times)? You could ask other large users about their experience. What are the step factors in scaling up? Can the cost of servers, hardware, licences, etc, be shared by other departments without creating conflicts?

5.   Are the basic functions, such as logging on, finding conferences, reading and sending messages, very easy and intuitive to use? If they are not, you are unlikely to get enough participants for successful conferencing, except in disciplines where users are very IT-literate, like computer science.

6.   Is the system widely accessible, available, cheap and easy to use for remote students and staff? Will enough of your e-moderators and students find it easy to use? What is the lowest technical specification that this system will work well on? If you have a variety of students and tutors using their own machines, many with older technologies, this is an important question. If you are using campus or corporate networks, can you ensure that all users will have appropriate and regular access to suitable PCs?

7.   Can users download a client for top functionality but also access the system from a browser wherever they are? Will it be easy to distribute pre-configured software to remote users – mailing out eight floppy discs is no longer acceptable! Will this distribution call for higher levels of technical support than are available to participants?

8.   Does the system require infrastructures, staffing or support that cannot be provided?

9.   Is the focus of the software on communication and/or knowledge sharing rather than the delivery of content?

10.   Is there e-mail on the same system as conferencing?

11.   Can users jump by hypertext link from messages to the Web? This is user-friendly and makes designing learning activities much easier. To what extent can activities take place entirely within a browser? This often helps with integration of course activities and resources, and students welcome it, but the system may lack certain functions that you value.

12.   Can remote participants work easily and effectively offline, thereby reducing telephone costs and enabling mobility?

13.   Is it culturally neutral (or at least has minimum cultural bias)?

14.   Does it provide good tools and techniques for e-moderators, such as message histories and a choice of icons? Are there good threading structures?

15.   Are there good document-handling tools?

16.   Is it possible to 'quote' easily from other people's messages?

17.   Does it have numerous features that are not needed? Does it include a lot of graphics? Users soon get bored with them. Similarly, does it look most like pages of text? If so, why not use print?

18.   Is there a personalization or customization function of some kind? At minimum, is there a way of bookmarking favourites or placing the most used conferences at a top level 'desktop'?

19.   Does it provide tracking and downloading of messages?

20. Are there simple and quick ways of personalizing the software, eg through a choice of icons or navigation devices?
21. Does it provide easy ways of grouping users? How can you provide for secure areas for collaborative groups and for e-moderators only, for example?
22. What are the direct, indirect, real, and per user costs? What are the possibly hidden costs for you (eg, a high level of training required for e-moderators)? What are the costs of training and maintaining technicians, administrators and help-desk staff? Will it be cost-effective and beneficial in your institution, your company, your context and for your purposes to outsource these functions and over what period of time?
23. Will the system save any time or shift time to cheaper people or leave more time for teaching and learning, at least in the medium term?
24. Will it provide a better service or learning environment for customers, students or clients compared to now? What is the added value compared to what you do now?
25. How will the system help raise standards of access and/or learning for students (or e-moderators/tutors) with disabilities?
26. Can the system be integrated with other online teaching, learning or assessment systems and applications? To what extent can existing teaching materials and approaches be adapted and incorporated into this system?
27. Do you need CMC within an 'overall online learning environment'? If so, how will it fit?

Fourthly, before you decide, do insist on trying the whole system on a small scale, preferably on your own network or dial up facilities, with some of your e-moderators and participants. There is another list of questions that e-moderators should consider:

28. Are you going to be in control of setting up and maintaining students' conferencing if you use this software?
29. Will you be able to change conferences, allow conferences to develop and evolve (or are you tied into pre-set structures)? What exactly are the limits and costs of this flexibility in practice? Can you easily create sub-conferences and delete unused ones?
30. Is there an easy way of accessing students' activities, eg when students last visited and what conferences they accessed?
31. Is summarizing and archiving a quick and easy function?
32. Are there really good 'threading' structures, since these may be the key to successful e-moderating?
33. Is it empowering for you and your participants or will any changes need to be filtered by people with greater technical skills or access than you?
34. Is there help available with teaching and other pedagogical techniques?
35. Do you think you can be trained as an e-moderator through the software environment itself?

There is a further set of questions that researchers and evaluators may want to ask:

36. Can this system be used as a tool for research, eg can it be adapted to collect quantitative research statistics and data (eg overall usage, log-in reports, etc), can messages easily be downloaded for analysis, are there any specific functions built in for researchers?
37. Does it provide for action research?
38. To what extent will it integrate with Web applications and research tools on your intranet, extranet or the Internet?

Resources for practitioners 2

Are you ready to work online?

To use the matrix below, look first at each application and place a cross in the box that best describes your current competence with that application. You should end up with 11 crosses in the boxes. To interpret your results, first count up how many crosses are above the line (ie top left-hand part) and how many are below (bottom right-hand part).

1. If you have four or more crosses under the line, you are likely to be able to get up to speed really quickly with CMC. I suggest you load up and start using online help.
2. If you have no crosses under the line, contact your local IT co-ordinator or try to find a suitable starter course for some preparation and coaching before you start.
3. If you have one to four crosses under the line, work through an online induction or network with experienced e-moderators before you begin e-moderating online.

Table II.1   *Competence and application*

Application	No Competence	Some Competence	Competence	High Competence
a Spreadsheets				
b Video or audio conferencing online				
c Database construction and use				
d Computer keyboard				
e Using Windows				
f Word Processors				
g Synchronous online chat				
h Information search and retrieval on the Internet				
i E-mail				
j Asynchronous discussion groups				
k Computer Mediated Conferencing				

Resources for practitioners 3

Keeping e-moderating costs down

Here are some useful tips to help keep e-moderating costs down:

1. Make clear decisions about roles and numbers of e-moderators that you will need and ensure they are trained in advance.
2. Train e-moderators online, rather than face to face.
3. Establish early on how much e-moderators should expect to do, and what are reasonable expectations on the part of students.
4. Keep your e-moderator support to students focused and specify what you expect them to do and when – if necessary, publish total number of hours per week or month available to participants.
5. Ensure that e-moderators can up- and download messages offline if they wish. Teach them how to use the CMC software to best advantage to save connection time.
6. Look into transfer of costs of hardware, software and connection to students, perhaps with grants for those unable to afford the cost, and to e-moderators, who may be able to count them as tools of their trade for tax purposes.
7. Set up good helpdesk and online support systems, and encourage competent students to support others, leaving more of your e-moderators' online time for learning related e-moderating.
8. Use existing resources and online constructed knowledge as much as possible rather than develop materials and/or pay for expensive third-party materials use.
9. Develop systems for reuse, where possible, of online conferencing materials.
10. Build up economies of scale as rapidly as possible – choose only systems that can be expanded cheaply.

Resources for practitioners 4

CMC users with disabilities

In the spirit of wide diversity and empowerment, it is good that the disabilities of CMC users with special needs are not usually obvious online. It is normally impossible to tell from the messages in a conference that a participant or an e-moderator has restricted vision, hearing or mobility, unless that person wishes to write about it. People who have problems with their speech or hearing are not at a disadvantage in text-based CMC. Those who have problems with their vision or physical movement may well find that the keyboard and screen prevent them for doing as much as they would like. Dyslexics still have some difficulties in CMC, even with electronic help available.

Blind and visually impaired users

Whereas many people with vision problems can learn to touch-type, they usually have problems in reading the screen. Windows software, for example, often requires precise placing of the mouse, even when keyboard commands are used wherever possible. An electronic screen-reader, that reads the text aloud at a steady pace and in a computer-generated voice, is valuable when long sections of text are onscreen, but useless when there is a diagram. The same is true of speech recognition software that enables users to speak the messages, for conversion into text by the computer. Taped instructions may help, but taped cassettes or material recorded on CD can prove difficult to manipulate.

Physically disabled users

Users who cannot freely move their hands and arms find that they cannot use the keyboard at a reasonable speed for CMC, even when the stiffness of the keys has been varied to suit. Speech recognition software may be better or semi-intelligent software that enables them to select whole words after the first few letters have been typed in. Exceptionally, CMC users may need single-switch devices to control modified computers and their peripherals.

Dyslexic users

Spelling and grammar checkers can be very helpful to dyslexic CMC users, particularly if their dyslexia is severe enough to put off non-dyslexic conference participants. The odd spelling or grammatical error worries nobody, but the condition may produce far worse effects.

Resources for practitioners 5

Online participant induction

These suggestions may appear 'over the top'. However, from my experience, it is easy to make wrong assumptions about learners' previous computer literacy, levels of online competence and early CMC behaviours and needs. The benefits of effective online induction and preparation are immense. When the course proper starts, the concentration of learners and teachers, participants and e-moderators can be on content, interaction and outcomes rather than passwords, software and lurking. Just as for a face-to-face group, making people comfortable and confident sets the tone for the course and leads to better learning.

Here are some suggestions for getting off to a good start:

1. Consider how much time you expect everyone will take to get up to speed – and double this.
2. Commence before the course proper starts (if you can, immediately you identify your participants).
3. Offer online induction for online learning.
4. Make it very clear to participants how the online induction and their use of CMC will lead to their increased success on the course. Some feedback suggests the need for serious 'luring' of online participants, eg shortcuts and ideas for time saving on the course, tips from course leaders about essential and 'nice to have' aspects of the course and the benefits of securing relevant wide-scale views and networking.
5. Get good helplines in place to solve technical and password problems.
6. Recognize that different people may need very different kinds of support at this stage (check this out – see Resources 2, 6, 7 and 13). Offer different streams and pathways for novices and the more experienced.

7. Ensure that each newcomer gets a friendly and individual greeting from an e-moderator (it's probably best to do this by e-mail to avoid clogging up the arrivals conferences).

8. Offer local support and motivation to get set up if you're dealing largely with remote users.

9. Offer the chance to conference in very small groups (up to 10) during the induction.

10. Remember that recent users of the induction programme (those who have progressed at least to stage 3, information exchange) make useful, patient and often enthusiastic supporters for newcomers. Perhaps set up an online mentoring system.

11. Keep navigation extremely simple and obvious, and provide direct pathways through the programme, stage by stage.

12. Keep the instructions very simple and as short as possible; use diagrams and illustrations that can be easily downloaded.

13. Focus induction activities on building confidence and socializing in the online environment.

14. Then focus on communicating and preparation for the course (not just the technology).

15. Ensure that there are worthwhile, authentic and relevant activities within the induction programme. Use inspiring questions to stimulate debate.

16. Don't assume that newcomers to the CMC system will find the answers they need to their queries in a mass of online instructions and FAQs – they need context-specific help (usually from a real person) in the early stages.

17. Ensure your e-moderators are friendly, supportive and that they visit their conferences often.

18. Ensure that each participant is pointed to permissible conduct, and codes of practice, and has a chance to discuss and explore their implications in the online environment.

19. Provide areas for 'junk' and practice messages.

20. Ensure that e-moderators and others with control of the look of the conferences leave them in an easy state for newcomers to navigate.

21. Track participation and follow up browsers and drop-outs by telephone or post.

Resources for practitioners 6

Supporting and developing CMC novices

Many participants in CMC are novices at communicating, teaching or learning online, even if they are familiar with computing. In the early days, they need special attention. Based on my research, e-moderators can expect three types of responses to CMC. I call these swimming, waving and drowning online.

The swimmers:

- dive in early;
- have conference-relevant experience, eg chat rooms on the Internet;
- are usually willing to help others;
- may become disruptive if they think the conferencing activities are not demanding enough;
- are likely to claim they know of better systems than the one you've chosen to use.

The wavers:

- need considerable help and encouragement to get started;
- depend on a telephone helpline or individual help even to appear online;
- arrive after the main group and need help in sifting through masses of messages;

- feel there is too little time to do everything;
- do very well and become enthusiasts once they've got logged on and are given support.

The drowners:

- find it very difficult indeed to log on and/or are reluctant to ask for or accept help;
- have little motivation to succeed;
- promise to log on but do not;
- complain at every opportunity that CMC is irrelevant or too time-consuming;
- find the relationship building and socializing online difficult, especially if they are used to taking a leading role in face-to-face groups;
- do better if a supportive *swimmer* is allocated to them as a mentor.

To convert wavers and drowners to swimmers:

- build 'scaffolding' – steps towards success and confidence – into your induction programme;
- provide social and test areas within the CMC environment where they can experiment and continue to build up their confidence;
- build onscreen displays that be navigated fairly intuitively, without constantly reading instructions;
- address student expectations when providing online resources and activities;
- offer parallel ways of working (ie via print or telephone as well as CMC) where access is an issue, but only for the shortest possible time because you need to build up a critical mass online quickly;
- provide a telephone helpline for resolving access and password problems;
- prepare step-by-step instructions on how to use the software and ask a naïve user to try them out before you put them on screen (have paper copies for those who want them);
- provide an individual e-mail welcome to each participant in response to his/her first CMC message and support each one in the early stages of learning conferencing;
- provide online help, instructions and an individual response from the course 'lifeguard' (possibly a postgraduate research student), backed up by support from recent novices, who can often help the new intake;
- engage as helpers individuals who have recently completed the e-moderator training or student induction (their help is highly valued in OUBS);
- provide students with full encouragement to learn by doing, by experimenting and by making mistakes in a supportive environment;

- emphasize the purposeful and relevant nature of conferencing for future learning on the course;
- e-moderate conferences often, with archiving of messages so that newcomers have only a few to read.

Resources for practitioners 7

Using the five-stage model

You will find below a summary of advice relevant to each of the five stages of the model. For each stage, there is advice on technical support you can provide, on helping participants to learn and on e-moderating in particular.

Stage 1: Access and motivation

Technical support

- Provide a helpline for password and access problems.
- Ensure new participants can read and know how to send messages as soon as they are online.
- Give great attention to precise detail in your written and onscreen instructions.
- Clarify the differences between e-mail and conferencing.
- Provide a printed manual for those who prefer one (may be copies of your own screen messages).

Motivating participants

- Recognize that taking part is an act of faith for most participants at this stage.
- Present (sell if necessary) CMC as a new way of learning through networking, emphasizing its importance as a communication and networking tool.
- Specify how CMC will be used in the course or programme.
- Ensure the 'look and feel' of your system is user-friendly for all comers.
- Try to make CMC fun, enticing and enjoyable.
- Assure novices that their fear and anxiety will be overcome by trying CMC.

E-moderating

- Acknowledge high levels of anxiety and lack of confidence in some participants may mean that some 'hand holding' is needed.
- Welcome participants individually.
- Constantly improve and update support materials.
- Keep the conference structure very clear and simple.
- Encourage participants to log on regularly, and do so yourself.

Stage 2: Socialization

Technical support

- Explain carefully how to save time and, if connecting through a phone line, money.
- Provide a 'lifeguard' – a person to e-mail for help online.
- Focus instructions on software facilities where participants can see immediate benefits, eg the address book, file attachment facility and shortcut keystrokes.
- Expect participants to believe there must be 'bugs' in the system since it does not behave how they expect it to, and be prepared to be very patient in providing support, explanation and resolution.
- Suggest to some participants that they should make a print-out from the screen, to have beside them when working through instructions for exercises.
- Navigating around the conferences will be easier if you use meaningful names and icons.
- Look out for those who lack confidence in manipulating Windows and be ready to help them.
- Some participants may need reassurance from you about spelling and typos.
- Don't alter the look of the desktop too often – novices get very worried by frequent changes in it.
- Know the rationale for your choice of CMC system, and the benefits of it for your participants, because some may make unfavourable comparisons with other more familiar software.

Learning

- Enhance participants' confidence in using CMC by praising their contributions.
- Offer ways for participants to benefit from reading about other people's CMC experience and problems.
- Explain the importance of acknowledging others online and set an example yourself.
- Point out why it is usually better to keep messages short and purposeful.
- Explain the benefits to participants of their working at their own pace.
- Ensure that ways for individuals to establish their identities online are used, eg explain how to read and post CVs (résumés).

E-moderating

- Check for any participants with relevant disabilities, however minor, and find out how you can help them.
- Use metaphors and straightforward explanation to provide bridges between familiar ways of communicating and CMC.
- Emphasize transferable skills and links to other experiences.
- Promote awareness of appropriate online communication styles.
- Encourage practice to reinforce developing skills.
- Allow lurking or browsing, without making this a moral issue.
- Offer structured exercises and activities to participants, especially those involved in finding online others with similar interests.
- Help participants with navigation and selection of conferences.
- Help participants to develop their own online identity.
- Allocate an online mentor to newcomers when possible.
- Aim to summarize and archive messages often, so that there are not more than 20 unread messages for any participant in any conference.

Stage 3: Information exchange

Technical support

- Offer advice and 'tips' for developing skills.
- Check that all basic skills are achieved.
- Encourage participants to see that the conferencing technology works and is quite simple to use.
- Provide information, for those who want it, about more sophisticated and advanced uses of software.

Learning

- Provide practical ways of sharing information online.
- Look for and build links with other media and processes in the course.

E-moderating

- Provide relevant and purposeful conferences.
- Deal with requests for information.
- Deal promptly with difficulties among participants, such as dominance, harassment, and perhaps excessive lurking.
- Offer tips and strategies for dealing with information overload.
- Provide a variety of conferences to suit different student needs.
- Set up useful activities and tasks – especially those not so easily or productively undertaken offline.

- Provide links into suitable electronic resources, eg Web sites and CD ROMs, to use as stimuli for conferences.
- Remind participants of the CMC protocols and guidelines if conferences get too busy or confused.

Stage 4: Knowledge construction

Technical support

- Encourage participants to become more technically independent and less handbook-dependent.
- Ensure good use of conference titles and icons.
- Promote benefits of CMC through explaining its technical aspects, eg its ease of use, asynchronicity and lack of dependence on a fixed location for each participant.
- Deal with any persistent technical problems.
- Ensure that all e-moderators have access and the skills for setting up conferences, creating sub-conferences, summarizing messages and creating archives.

Learning

- Pose insightful questions and give participants time to reflect and respond.
- Encourage participants to contribute to the conferences, not merely read them.
- Ensure there is no domination of conferences by one or two individuals.
- Explore every opportunity for online collaboration with others.

E-moderating

- Be prepared to explain and clarify the e-moderating role to participants (especially if they are still expecting 'the answers' from you at this stage).
- Work on developing your skills in e-moderating for knowledge construction.
- Share with other e-moderators insights into how to deal with online 'problem participants' and 'problem groups', in case you encounter them.
- Encourage full contribution and participation by students.
- Know when to stay silent for a few days.
- Be prepared to value every participants' contribution but summarize, summarize, summarize.
- Be ready to hand out specific e-moderating tasks to participants, to give them a chance to experience e-moderating for themselves.
- Close off any unused or unproductive conferences and create new ones.

Stage 5: Development

Technical

- Ensure that links exist from conferences to the Internet, library, etc.
- Ensure that selected participants can be given access to set up and e-moderate their own conferences.

Learning

- Enable participants to offer help to others or to become e-moderators.
- Provide opportunities for reflection on the what and how of learning online.
- Provide opportunities for development and progress.

E-moderating

- Expect and welcome challenges of all kinds (the system, the conferences, the conclusions).
- Ensure that appropriate evaluation, monitoring and reflection on your own practice occurs.
- Encourage participants to reflect on CMC by providing conference areas to discuss the impact of online networking for learning.
- Explore comparisons with face-to-face learning.
- Look for those with good online skills and communication styles, and encourage them to support others.

Resources for practitioners 8

Evaluating participation on CMC – ideas for e-moderators

Selecting objectives to evaluate

CMC is an important part of the new approach to online learning; therefore you should consider very carefully the objectives you want to use in evaluating your success with it. These objectives may be different from ones you have used in the past (Duchastel, 1997):

- Be explicit from the start about your instructional strategies and the ideals and values behind your use of CMC.
- Provide ways for participants to collaborate on authentic and relevant activities through CMC.
- Encourage students to use conference messages as data or illustration in assignments.
- Look at the processes of learning rather than testing the content transmitted.
- Explore the impact of conferencing on skills such as reflection on practice, meta–cognition and practical outcomes.
- Integrate course activities and assignments with the use of CMC and look at students' learning as a whole, because you'll have trouble if you try to separate out the influence of CMC alone.
- Accept diversity of outcomes rather than demanding uniform learning.
- Consider whether knowledge is being created and disseminated rather than information merely communicated.

- Consider how well tasks and outcomes have been achieved.
- Consider the success of teams rather than only that of individuals.
- Encourage and reward cross-boundary, cross-disciplinary achievements and complexity.
- Use the online medium for review and assessment rather than reverting to old ways such as closed book, paper-based examinations.
- Use online feedback questionnaires to get fast and effective feedback.

Evaluating what?

You may want to collect data from your conferences for evaluation purposes. Make sure you respect the privacy of conference messages. Avoid dropping in unannounced, and seek permission if you want to quote a message from the conferences (the copyright belongs to the originator of each message, strictly speaking).

Here is a list of some questions you could explore:

1. How many of your participants log on at least once, read and contribute? It used to be said that a third of CMC students read and contribute, a third only read messages and a third neither read nor contribute because they never access the conferences. Is this true for you?
2. What helps to motivate participants online, what do they enjoy and benefit from, what encourages them to contribute? Can you develop a control group for comparisons? When you change something in CMC, try to measure the impact, which can be quite large.
3. Do those that do not take part in CMC participate less in the course overall or are they choosing alternative means of communication? Do more of those who fail to take part in CMC drop out or achieve lower results?
4. Who is relating to whom and in what way? What requests are there for setting up new conferences or other online activities?
5. Do the conferences provide learning to those for whom it was intended? Or are they providing learning only to 'early adopters'? Are the benefits spread across all learners? Do some groups benefit more than others? Check whether there are improvements in student learning, as opposed to enthusiasm about the novelty of working with new media.
6. What are the trade-offs on conferencing? What is not happening that did before?
7. Does the five-stage model (Figure 2.1) hold true for your learners in your CMC?
8. Are costs shifted onto the students by CMC? Is this worth it for them, and for you?
9. Can you use message history and log-on facilities to spot and support students who are struggling?

10. Are there differences in results between structured and unstructured, well and less well e-moderated conferences?
11. How much time do participants spend on CMC? How does this compare with your traditional ways of learning and interaction? If it is more, or less, is this good or bad?

Resources for practitioners 16 gives you some ideas for analyzing types of messages from participants.

Resources for practitioners 9

Training e-moderators

1. Ensure that the trainee e-moderators experience CMC as learner before they start e-moderating for real.
2. Ensure that they undertake all or most of the programme in the online environment itself – make it a real experience.
3. Keep the focus of the programme on the development of the trainees as e-moderators – the training is about e-moderating rather than about the software or other aspects of their training better dealt with elsewhere.
4. Keep the training as simple as such a focus will allow – don't over-complicate it.
5. Provide an environment suited to trainees with a wide range of prior skills (or none).
6. Check the training programme thoroughly before the programme goes live – use a novice for a final check rather than an expert, but give the trainers an opportunity to familiarize themselves with the programme in advance.
7. Provide the minimum of print-based materials consistent with helping trainees to get started and make sure that those materials match what is on screen.
8. Make clear to the trainees how much time you expect them to spend on the programme.
9. Make sure the training programme is accessible 'any time, any place'.
10. Build in help with the software and the system as much as you can to control frustration.
11. Enable trainees to acquire skills in using the software as they gradually build up their understanding of the online environment.
12. Ensure your trainers of the trainers – your e-moderators of the trainee e-moderators (we call them convenors) – model exemplary e-moderating skills in the training programme.

13. Include strategic knowledge (how will I work with my students?) as well as declarative knowledge and procedural knowledge (availability and capacity of the software and the system).
14. Offer plenty of opportunity for the trainees to explore their attitudes to CMC and its meaning for their own teaching.
15. Ensure the trainees have opportunities to interact with each other.
16. Make the trainees aware of the goals of the programme all the way through it.
17. Use familiar metaphors for explaining aspects of CMC and e-moderating.
18. Try and spot trainees needing more help and offer it promptly (see 'swimmers, wavers and drowners' in Resources for practitioners 6).
19. Build reflection on e-moderating practice into your training programme.
20. Monitor the work of e-moderators and use feedback to improve your training programme.
21. Ensure that ongoing development of trained e-moderators is available and build an online community of e-moderators' conferences after the training programme has been completed.

Resources for practitioners 10

E-moderation principles for productive conferencing

1. Make sure you are in the conference with welcoming messages before the participants arrive.
2. Provide time for participants to become familiar with the conferences in the programme, preferably in advance.
3. Create structures and expectations for conferences.
4. Set clear objectives and clarify expectations for your online groups.
5. Provide enough, but not too much, intervention (not more than one in four messages from you).
6. Build up your conferences through stages of individual welcome, social community building as quickly and effectively as possible, but never leave these stages out.
7. Be flexible, responsive and innovative to conference design and development.
8. Be inclusive of all and value all participants.
9. Be satisfied with one or two key points emerging from the discussion.
10. Find the unifying threads in a discussion, build, weave and re-present ideas constantly (present and be comfortable with conflicting opinions).
11. Accommodate lurkers or browsers, at least for a while as they may have their reasons but e-mail or phone them with support if they persist in non-participation.
12. Be patient and persistent, especially with novice users.
13. Let participants know if you are going to be offline for a while.
14. Model behaviours and ways of communicating online.
15. Be clear how often you are logging on and what participants can expect from you.

16. Work towards Level five behaviours, eg request reflection and comment on the learning occurring online.
17. Pace the conferencing realistically.
18. Change inappropriate titles and headings of messages (with e-mail explanation).
19. Move messages in the wrong conference (with e-mail explanation to the contributor).
20. Deal quietly and privately with anyone dominating the discussion – ask them to reflect before responding.
21. Conclude discussions before they peter out – if a conference flags, delete it (with an online explanation) and start another.
22. Encourage participants to use conference messages as data or for illustration in assignments.
23. Collect participants' views and feedback on your own performance through online mechanisms.

Resources for practitioners 11

Techniques for
CMC structures

The following table details some techniques for CMC structures.

Table II.2 *Techniques for CMC structures*

No.	Type	Purpose	Ideal Student Numbers	Conference Construction	Time	E-Moderate	E-Moderator Action
1	Location Groups	• Support for groups that may also meet face to face • Provide noticeboard for changes, reminders and tips • Provide support for self-help groups and socializing • Post notes and handouts	• Approx 3–20 for research and discussion • Max 9 for collaborative working	• 2 sub-conferences – create others to serve interest later	• Conference lasts: 4 weeks to 12 months • Keep messages for: 8 weeks • Chat conference 14 days only	• Twice weekly, more often for busy conference • Keep messages	• provide ideas • provide pointers out to study material and other teaching and learning devices • look for 'gaps' in knowledge or understanding • set up sub-conferences if small interest groups emerge • use e-mail until conference established
2	Continuing collaborative working	Follow up on residential school activities	6–30 6–12 ideal	Keep structure flat	For as long as interest remains (usually until after exam or other assessed elements are completed)	• Weekly • Keep messages for 4 weeks	• appoint student as e-moderator • housekeep
3	Online 'market research'	• Data and opinion gathering 'ie collaborative research' usually for a purpose eg use in assignments • Collaborative working	10–50	'Lobby' with questions Sub-conferences for data input	3–4 weeks	• Twice weekly more often if possible • Keep messages for: length of conference and until assessed elements are completed	• ask key questions • designate key actions • follow up non-respondents

4	Online tutorials	• Contextualize and personalize course material • Enhance appreciation of concepts in terms of student work • Tutorials for students all working in same industry, corporate or culture	10–20 with conferencing experience	Lobby plus two sub-conferences – one for depository of concepts and Resources, one for discussion	Ideal time: 6 weeks	• Twice weekly • Keep messages for: length of conference but summarize and archive discussion every 20 messages	• provide information eg 6 key words • ask questions, eg what happens at your place of work? • compare with own experience, eg country with UK • direct questions via e-mail to non-participants and ask them to post answer in conference
5	Vast resource recognition	• Getting to know others on line • Recognizing resource of others available online	10–100	Lobby plus 'answers' sub-conference	2–3 weeks at commencement of course	• At beginning and end of period • Keep messages for: Length of conference	• pre-conference: look through all résumés online and pick out key questions • post questions on conference • offer prize or feedback for participant reaching highest score • post 'answers'
6	Debating	• Stimulating debate • Widening viewpoints • Encouraging structured participation	6 to take roles Up to 50 browsing and discussion	Lobby plus two sub-conferences 'for' and 'against'	4 weeks	• Twice weekly daily for busy conferences • Keep messages for: 6 weeks	• seek 6 participants to argue for particular positions (3 for and 3 against) • e-moderate post debate discussion • offer 'spreadsheet' detailing for and against votes

Table II.2 *Continued*

No.	Type	Purpose	Ideal Student Numbers	Conference Construction	Time	E-Moderate	E-Moderator Action
7	Assignments	Prepare for assignment	10–50	Lobby plus one or two sub conferences for discussion	4 weeks before assessment is due	• Archive after 20 messages • Keep messages until: Day assignment is due	• Post up question • set up and stay silent • summarize overall discussion at end
8	Master Classes	Enable large scale access to expert eg course team member or external	Up to 2000	Lobby plus number of subgroups enabling smaller scale discussion	4 weeks, link with course	• Often–daily, archive every 2 days • Keep messages for: 2 weeks – summaries	• set up • support topic expert • suggest key concepts • reinforce discussion • focus on process/presentation of conference • archive after 20 messages
9	Collaboration	Online group collaboration	5–20	Small sub-conference for specific groups	4 weeks	• Twice weekly • Keep messages for: 6 weeks	• encourage free exchange of information • e-mail and follow up browsers • summarize
10	Deepen Understanding	Student collaboration for deepening understanding of course concepts and for exam revision	Up to 50 (less if all fully participating)	Lobby two sub-conferences Two – one for summarizing, one for discussion of concept	4 weeks Start and finish according to course calendar (ie to match course)	• Twice weekly • Keep messages for: 6 weeks	• put chunks of course or articles online • invite students to summarize from their perspective • summarize in lobby lead discussion

#	Name	Number	Purpose	Structure	Duration	Frequency	E-moderator role
11	'Beyond' for Specialists	5–20	'Beyond the basic for specialists', eg International banking for accountant/finance people studying the MBA	Lobby plus one or two subs for discussion	4 weeks	• Every two days • Keep messages for: 4 weeks	• enables expert to start topic off, eg her research area/ ask for views • e-moderate discussion between peers (use experienced student e-moderator)
12	Post exam	20 maximum	• Support 'post exam' conference depression • Keep students in touch between courses • provide some fun and learning • provide skills practice in conference and spreadsheets • eg fantasy investment club	Lobby plus one or two subs	5–6 weeks	• Twice weekly • Keep messages for: 6 weeks	• provide fantasy money, eg £20,000 • answer students' questions • provide daily news items • provide weekly results
13	Revision	Up to 500	Support revision and preparation for exam	Lobby plus sub conference containing each of the questions from the SEP. Can also be done with key concepts from blocks of the course	6 weeks to finish day before exam	• 3 times a week • Keep until conference Up to 30 in each sub conference then summarize/ archive	• post an example question into each of the sub conferences • ask for key concepts from the course for each question • Facilitate discussion on answering questions

Table II.2 *Continued*

No.	Type	Purpose	Ideal Student Numbers	Conference Construction	Time	E-Moderate	E-Moderator Action
14	Interest	Major interest groups	30 fully participating in each sub-conference (more if you can tolerate browsers)	Lobby to welcome all students (up to 1500) Directions to join individual sub-conferences (up to 50)	6 weeks	• Twice weekly • Keep messages for: 8 weeks	• allocate each student to sub-conference • summarize input every 10–15 participants • input current events that contribute, link to relevant outside material • process facilitate – maintain momentum • summarize frequently
15	More deepen	• Active student engagement of material • Deepening understanding of course concepts	Any but divided into 6–8s	Sub-conferences to enable small 'cell' groups, easy access	2–3 weeks	• Actively and often eg twice weekly • Keep messages for: 4 weeks	• define task and time • provide early direction then stay 'hands off' • e-mail individuals not participating • share expertise • challenge • test • reflect
16	Peer groups	• Application of course to own work through peer group discussion • Networking	6–20	Lobby plus discussion sub-conferences	6 weeks	• Process reinforcement • Keep messages for: 6 weeks	• emphasis confidentially and support • provide questionnaires format/ networking exercises

#	Name	Purpose	Size	Structure	Duration	Frequency	Actions
17	Idea generate	Generation of large numbers of ideas	20–100	One main conference	4 weeks	• E-moderate twice weekly • Keep messages until summary available	• set up • emphasize 'rules of brainstorming' (ie that no discussion/evaluation) at this stage • encourage participation – ask to discuss elsewhere • summarize and categorize all contributions at end
18	Communities	large scale course community building	any	Lobby plus emergent sub-groups as desired	6–9 months	• Daily • Keep messages for: 4 weeks	(team of e-moderators) • list e-moderators and course team at beginning • constant archiving and threading • daily 'tips'/news flashes • course team involvement
19	Problems	support for problem solving	12's	Lobby plus sub-groups to take 12	4 weeks	• Twice weekly • Keep messages for: 6 weeks	• invite students to post 'problems' • invite up to 12 participants into sub-conference • keep hands off but summarize at end • follow up with 'problem owner'
20	Fun	• Fun • Gaining CMC experience (eg online wine tasting, line dancing, fantasy investing)	20	Sub groups for those who want to take part	4 weeks max	• Occasionally • Keep messages for: 4 weeks	• get ideas • set up • close down
21	Self-Help	Student self-help group	3–20	Lobby plus two sub-groups	4 weeks to 12 months	• Weekly • Keep messages for 4 weeks	Housekeeping

Resources for practitioners 12

Conference housekeeping

The conferencing environment needs to be looked after, in much the same way as your house, apartment or teaching environment, in order to keep it serviceable. These factors are largely 'hygiene' factors, ie will be invisible if they are working well. Without them, many conferences have foundered. Without 'housekeeping' your loftier or more creative teaching and learning online goals are unlikely to be achievable. Many studies have shown that small changes in housekeeping make a considerable difference! Make these protocols clear to your e-moderators:

1. Decide whether conferences and their sub-sets will be set up in advance, or whether you will allow topics and sub-conferences to 'emerge' over time, – and housekeep accordingly, so that the conferences operate how participants expect.

2. Allow interesting and relevant topics to 'emerge' from participants at various times, create sub-conferences to support emergent topics, and delete dormant conferences to make virtual space for them.

3. E-moderators need to visit often (agree how often) and notify participants if they are likely to be offline for more than a week or so (lack of appearance online mystifies and disturbs other users). Ask a colleague e-moderator to visit your conference whilst you are away.

4. Teams of e-moderators should work together to ensure regular responses to participants and maintenance of conferences.

5. Create and maintain good 'layout' of onscreen access conferences, very easy navigation around them and the quick closing and deleting of inactive conferences to keep the screen as clear as possible.

6. Summarize, delete or archive messages so that no more than around 20 messages in any one conference or sub-conference are active at any one

time. This avoids participants being overwhelmed upon visiting a conference after a few days.

7. In many software packages, how the e-moderator leaves the screen when logging off will be how it will appear to users of the conference when they log on. Leave the screen as they would expect to find it.

Resources for practitioners 13

Understanding lurkers

First, identify the types of lurkers you have and appropriate responses. There are three main kinds:

1. Those still trying to find out how to use the system, who lack access, skills or confidence to participate (ie those operating at levels one and two in the five-stage model). Check whether they need help to log on, or simply greater motivation or encouragement through one-to-one contact with you, by e-mail or telephone, or perhaps some written instructions.
2. The sponge – people who are needing a bit of time to come to terms with the environment, norms and ways of communicating online – ie those at levels two and three in the model. Give them time and support and they should start to take part.
3. The silent thief/freeloader – people happy to use other people's contributions rather than feeling the need to contribute. These people need a reason – even a requirement – to take part.

Here are some strategies:

1. Check that all participants know how to post and 'reply' to messages.
2. Provide a test area and an arrivals area.
3. Check that you have a free-flowing or social conferencing area.
4. Give participants plenty of time to become used to the online environment before insisting that they post their responses.
5. Check across all your conferences – your lurkers may be participating (and using their time and energy) in a different conference from where you were expecting them to be.
6. Reduce the number of messages in each conference – there'll be less to read so they'll be more likely to reply.

7. Check you have a critical mass for the purpose of a conference (less than 6 participants or more than 15 active participants is likely not to work well, depending on the online activity).
8. Try some humour rather than anger (eg don't be a lurker – be a worker).
9. Check whether one or two individuals are dominating the conference – and deal tactfully with them to create a more open and equal environment.
10. Provide a structured evaluation questionnaire or an area for reflections and/or comments (some lurkers prefer safety in structure).
11. Explain to active participants what you are trying to do.
12. Allocate active participants to lurkers as mentors.
13. Rename 'lurkers' as 'browsers' and worry less about them.

Resources for practitioners 14

Boosting CMC participation

I'm often asked, 'In what ways can e-moderators make learners participate in CMC?' Well of course you can't make anyone do anything, but you can ensure CMC is attractive and worthwhile for as many people as possible and reduce known 'turn-offs'. Here is a list of ideas from experienced e-moderators for you to consider. The ideas are divided into 'carrots' (encouragement) or 'sticks' (penalties for not participating).

Carrots

Sell benefits

- Promote the benefits of CMC at face-to-face meetings with demonstrations if possible.
- Get others to explain how they were once online novices and their satisfaction of achieving online communication skills.
- Ensure the benefits for learning are explained.
- Explain how easy CMC is.
- Explain the support available online.
- Explain that many people find CMC reduces panic as assessments and tests come nearer.
- Explain the opportunities for making contacts and friendships online.
- Explain CMC's role in providing confirmation of one's own ideas.
- Explain that it will help with everyday life skills, eg e-business and e-commerce.

Add value to the learning methods

- Provide online feedback on students' progress.
- Give recognition (public and private) to those successfully contributing to CMC.
- Give opportunities for individuals to explore own ideas and influence others through CMC.
- Ensure that CMC enhances understanding of course content.

Build contacts and communities

- E-moderate most carefully to ensure inclusion of all, lack of discrimination and celebration of diversity.
- Ensure CMC enables the building of a community of peers (not only teacher–student contact).
- Ensure conferences give access to the knowledge of others in a distributed network.
- Give access to known experts in the field.
- Provide activities that are not available or possible except online (eg large-scale but easy research).
- Provide specialist contact, eg industry or interest groups.
- Provide conferences that enable individuals to 'keep up' with news about peers and competitors.
- Ensure everyone has a chance to contribute, ie personal visibility.
- Ensure academics, instructors, teaching assistants log on as well as learners.
- Ensure social and friendship building conferences are available.
- Provide ongoing online contact after the course is over.
- Provide for self-help groups and voluntary group working.
- Allow for lurking, give time for participants to develop.
- Keep the purpose of all conferences clear and focused and constantly reiterated throughout online activities or discussions.
- At level 4 (knowledge construction) provide for working through new problems, insist on valuing all contributions and no 'right' answer, creating and making meaning from all contributions, excellent e-moderating, sharing good practice.
- Provide online tutorials and support on course material that has proved difficult or challenging.
- Run online tutorial sessions before assessments or exams (watch them flock in!).

Assessment

- Provide extra marks for participation or percentage of marks of total score.
- Consider peer endorsements based on quality of contributions to discussion (for further ideas see Resources for practitioners 8).

- Monitor and publish longer-term performance, especially if working online leads to success on the course, linked to online participation of students.

Sticks (try to convert sticks into carrots)

Sticks to use

- Make other ways of achieving the same learning or assessment more difficult to undertake.
- Insist on online participation having a direct relationship to assessment, ie assessed components of course cannot be completed without CMC participation.
- Provide some key pieces of information online, ie only way of accessing.
- Enforce compulsory group working by making completion of projects impossible otherwise.
- Post relevant and useful information online for short periods only (ie an incentive to log on at a particular time).
- Set very clear and structured deadlines for submission of online work.

Sticks to avoid

- Discrimination of all kinds;
- Technical and access difficulties (for participants and e-moderators);
- Attacks from active contributors on lurkers;
- Lack of academic recognition or credit given for work on CMC;
- Bullying of any kind (including by e-moderators);
- Exclusion from the course because of lack of online participation.

Resources for practitioners 15

Knowledge sharing and construction

It is at Stage 4, Knowledge sharing and construction, that CMC has the most to offer teaching and learning. To achieve these, e-moderators need to do the following:

1. Get technical questions out of the way before the real start of the course.
2. Make clear what the e-moderator's role is, ie to collect and represent participants' views.
3. Create a setting and an atmosphere where differences as well as similarities are appreciated, and where disagreements are seen as an opportunity to learn.
4. Be an equal participant in the conference.
5. Avoid directive interventions and 'right answer' responses.
6. Encourage and support other participants in the e-moderating role.
7. Stimulate the debate, offer ideas, and offer resources (rather than 'the answers').
8. Provide 'sparks' (comments or stimulating questions that will prompt responses).
9. Be prepared to collate carefully, weave together and represent the discussion, ie undertake summarizing and modelling activities.
10. Intervene at the right point in time in the debate and appreciate the delicate balance between 'holding back' and intervening.
11. Share your range of experience but avoid overload or overwhelming participants.
12. Make explicit to participants that their contributions are wanted and valued (and that CMC is not a test).
13. Be careful to acknowledge and be inclusive of all contributions.

14.   Be clear to the group about what additional 'powers' you have as e-moderator, and the circumstances in which you would use them. (Some participants believe that e-moderators sneak around online.)

15.   Be very tolerant of natural twists and turns of discussion – it's unlikely to go the way you originally expected!

16.   Use CMC software that supports good threading and weaving and searchable archives.

17.   Look for evidence of knowledge construction and reward it (rather than expecting specific outcomes).

18.   Accept variety and diversity in responses and reward these.

19.   Reward task accomplishments rather than test for information recall.

20.   Assess co-operative, group, collaborative and team outcomes, rather than individuals' ones, wherever possible.

Resources for practitioners 16

Conference text examples

If you have never taken part in a computer conference, the following three examples should give you something of the 'look' and 'feel' of being in one. They are extracts from conferences associated with the Open University MBA course, B820 *Strategy*. They have had to be harshly pruned to reduce the amount of space they take up in the book. A live conference may be a little more messy and variable than these.

You may find helpful my nine categories for analyzing such conferences, because they make it easier to see what's happening in the debate. Look for the code numbers [in square brackets] as you read the exchanges. You could use these categories yourself in conferences that you e-moderate.

Conference analysis

Individual thinking
1   Offering up ideas or resources and inviting a critique of them
2   Asking challenging questions
3   Articulating, explaining and supporting positions on issues
4   Exploring and supporting issues by adding explanations and examples
5   Reflecting on and re-evaluating personal opinions
Interactive thinking
6   Offering a critique, challenging, discussing and expanding ideas of others
7   Negotiating interpretations, definitions and meanings
8   Summarizing and modelling previous contributions
9   Proposing actions based on ideas that have been developed

Example I

This extract derives from a sub-conference on strategy in the Voluntary Sector. Note particularly how each participant contributes his or experience and views. These participants are effectively using the technique of quoting the question to which they are responding in their first line of their message. The e-moderator is active in proposing challenging questions and throwing out ideas to get the conference started, but one of the students (PD) also helps stimulate responses and discussion.

There were nine individuals in the conference and the e-moderator is HB. The heading for each message indicates the initials of the sender and the date of the message.

PD 31 May

Thank you Susan, Diane, Cara and Tom. At last I feel we might be getting somewhere.

Anthony how are you?

If I were a profit-making organization providing services to a voluntary organization I would regard myself as a supplier and expect to get paid (mutually beneficial exchange). Much as I might like to do voluntary work, I can't afford to. My continued co-operation is dependent on the voluntary organization's ability to pay. [1] If I were influenced and persuaded by the not-profit motives and values of the charity (identification with norms, values and beliefs), I would become a donor or supporter. Is there a distinction between these categories? Would I be right in saying a donor provides cash whereas a supporter gives time or effort free of charge? [2] Excuse my ignorance, but what are Trustees? Are these the people who own the assets of the organization? What happens to the assets if the organization was to collapse? [2] And who are the customers? If the primary objectives are aimed at social good, are the customers the ones in direct receipt of the benefits provided by the organization, even though they may not be required to pay for these benefits? Or is it the state as Diane says, or are the donors customers, giving money in return for what? [2]
   Regards, Paul

HB 31 May

PD writes:

Excuse my ignorance, but what are Trustees? Are these the people who own the assets of the organization? What happens to the assets if the organization was to collapse? [1]

Trustees own the assets of the organization and act as Directors would in a Limited Company, ie they are the Senior Management – even thought they will not necessarily be managers in the day-to-day sense of the word. [4]

And who are the customers? If the primary objectives are aimed at social good, are the customers the ones in direct receipt of the benefits provided by the organization, even though they may not be required to pay for these benefits? Or is it the state, as Diane says, or are the donors customers, giving money in return for what? [1]

Good question Paul. I have seen it suggested that charities have bi-focal stakeholders, ie when looking at funding the donors are the customers and the receivers are internal stakeholders. – When providing a service the receivers are external stakeholders and the donors internal (what they want will affect what the organization does). This for me is part of the fascination of the sector. That unlike the For-Profit and Public Sectors the use of stakeholder analysis is far more complex. Maybe we might develop this issue further [4].

Cheers, Haydn

CL 1 June

Identifying the main stakeholders will surely be part of the 'marketing audit'. [6]

The ICT required by each of these groups will be different – would it be an idea to 'segment' the market according to stakeholder needs rather than on the functional basis I suggested earlier? [5]

Would it be a good idea to decide on a process of how we tackle and construct the work for this Tutor Marked Assignment? [7] In reality we would be setting up project teams if we were embarking on a major market development? [9] Maybe there are those of you who have had experience in setting up such project teams – could you suggest a way forward? [9] Can we divide the task up in some way.

Any thoughts or suggestions?? Cara

PD 1 June

HB writes:

I have seen it suggested that charities have bi-focal stakeholders, ie when looking at funding the donors are the customers and the receivers are internal stakeholders. – When providing a service the receivers are external stakeholders and the donors internal (what they want will affect what the organization does). [4]

Can a stakeholder be regarded as a customer if they don't have to pay? [1] How about the idea that the receivers are the product, ie what the organization does, and the donors are the customers, ie those who buy and pay for the product. [*1*]

HB 2 June

PD writes:

Can a stakeholder be regarded as a customer if they don't have to pay?

Yes, if their attitudes and feelings affect how the organization makes decisions. [3]
How about the idea that the receivers are the product, ie what the organization does, and the donors are the customers ie those who buy and pay for the product. [7]
What the organization does and who it does it for are not necessarily the same: as you might seem to imply. So is the product what it does, or for whom it does it? [7]
Cheers, Haydn

MK 2 June

PD writes:

Can a stakeholder be regarded as a customer if they don't have to pay?'

Haydn says 'yes' and I have to agree and would cite the following examples. *(Message gives examples from experience)* [4] Hope this helps. Meredith

PD 2 June

HB writes:

What the organization does and who it does it for are not necessarily the same: as you might seem to imply. So is the product what it does, or for whom it does it? [6]

A customer is one who buys a product or service.
A donor is one who gives.
A receiver is one who accepts/receives. [6]
Is the customer concept relevant to the voluntary sector? Could this be a case of force fit by the application of marketing logic and the dominant business paradigm? [6]
I am of the opinion that we could drop 'customers' from the stakeholder framework and substitute 'donors' and 'receivers' in their place. This would make five forces analysis more relevant, swapping 'customer power' for 'donor power' and 'receiver power' (6 forces analysis?) [7]
Regards Paul

HB 3 June

PD writes:

I am of the opinion that we could drop 'customers' from the stakeholder framework and substitute 'donors' and 'receivers' in their place. This would make five forces analysis more relevant, swapping 'customer power' for 'donor power' and 'receiver power' (6 forces analysis?)

I can see the roots of your approach Paul, but am not convinced. I think the Voluntary Sector does treat donors as customers and receivers as customers, but at different times and in different focuses. I suspect we might be seeing the difficulty with the sector as an analysis – ie that it has two sets of stakeholders depending if you are looking at sources of funds or object of funds. Again they have two markets – to be seen to do the right thing and to gain attention to what is done. They also have difficulty with management based on the finance driven fund-raising (my own area of experience) and the delivery arm, whose mission aims and objectives cannot often be reconciled. Internal stakeholders are therefore also more fragmented than in other organizations. [7]
Who else would like to reflect on this dichotomy and its impact on the analysis of the sector? [2]
   Cheers, Haydn

(There were around 20 responses to this question.)

PD 4 June

There were some interesting comments on staff remuneration in the early chatter topics. [8]

- Unremunerated non-executive directors or management committee members. . . often bring their own personal agendas. DB
- Voluntary sector employees. . . offer them better salaries and conditions because we are not creaming a profit off before salaries.
- Their remuneration reflects the fact that they have some additional, say ideological, stakeholder interest in the company – they aren't paid the going rate because they care.

Do voluntary sector employees/managers have to take vows of poverty and commit to the ideology of the organization? [2]
Could we explore this further? There may be implications for the balance of stakeholder power and the effectiveness of strategies – question (b). [7]
Regards Paul

SD 5 June

Paul asks – Do voluntary sector employees / managers have to take vows of poverty and commit to the ideology of the organization?

Could we explore this further? There may be implications for the balance of stakeholder power and the effectiveness of strategies – question (b).

I don't take vows of poverty – I see myself as an earning employee, but I work for a large org which is well off – some employees of small and struggling organizations I know do work above and beyond the call of duty. . . voluntary organizations tend not to be unionized, but why would probably be a complex question. [3]

However, although I see myself as someone doing a fair day's work etc, I do sign up to the mission and values of the organization and indeed the organization expects congruence between my personal and professional values and theirs – there is a kind of symbolic signing up to these when appointed. . . This certainly seems different to the organizational 'values' thinking in our course which expected organizations would sustain considerable differences between personal/organizational values, though would expect loyalty when on the job to organizational expectations. . . [3]

I'm not sure how that relates to power of stakeholders, but employees are a considerably important lot. . . Perhaps more so than Trustees in some voluntary organizations. . . Though this gets complicated because in some voluntary organizations Trustees are also users of services (eg self-help networks like MIND) [4]

I think? / Susan

SD 5 June

Re donors and customers. . .

I think of resource providers (donors, individual and corporate and grant makers) (and purchasers of services)

And Service Users (receivers of services who may or may not make a contribution towards cost but usually do not) [3]

Donors are also customers of our objectives, donating fulfils their giving intentions, and they can shop around to find the organization that meets this best . . .

Purchasers of services are also customers – mostly public bodies who buy our service provision to help them fulfil their duties. . .

Then again some public bodies also grant aid the Voluntary Organization's – especially small ones – with no expectation other then the Voluntary Organization will carry on. . . [7]. . . Susan

PD 8 June

Thanks to all who have so far responded to my plea for ideas on stakeholders. Please keep your thoughts coming!
How significant are 'lenders' to the voluntary sector? Do voluntary organizations take out loans like private companies, and end up having to raise funds to pay bank interest?
And who is the competition? Is there direct head on competition like Pepsi and Coke?
Or is it more sideways competition, competing for lottery money or for the pound in my pocket against other things I might spend it on? [2]
   Regards Paul

CL 7 June

Paul asks 'who is the competition?'
I think competition in the VOLUNTARY SECTOR comes in several forms: Rival fund-raising activities, rival bids for contracts, rival bids for grants eg the national lottery, other service providers, selling its products merchandise (charity shops), education. I'm sure there's more!! Does that help? [4]
   Cara

PD 8 June

Paul asks for scoring of stakeholders on the power matrix. [1]

At this point the conference continued with each participant contributing his or her views on a structured audit based on a simple model from the course material. Another 35 messages were posted. The conference ran for around a week, culminating in the entire group submitting individual assignments.

Example 2

This is a second example of knowledge construction through CMC, this time from the conference on the Brewing Sector. There were 10 participants. The e-moderator was AK. The sequence begins with AM's message on 30th May entitled 'Innovation'. The participants actively comment and build on each other's contributions while giving their own views and sources of information.

AM 30 May

Hi, does anyone else out there see the changes in the UK Pub & Brewery business as an example of innovation (see book 6)? [2]
This I would suggest strategies change in two ways.

1. The arrival and rapid growth of the new Pub retailers.
2. The growing importance of Brands and concepts to fill the gap of the businesses which had to be disposed of. [3]

I believe that the second point is worth further debate as I think it is the key issue which will split the market in the next 10 years, with the big players at one end and the smaller regional brewer at the other. [6]
Regards Arnold's suggestion: Meredith & Ben how about a meet in one of our great pubs shortly? [1] Anthony

MW 31 May

Arnold, I believe the line you are proposing about the wider moves and consequent strategic ramifications are the best use of this conference. [6]
While I admire the effort of those who are digging out statistics and interviewing micro brewers I cannot help but think that is all far too detailed . . . the one thing this course has brought home to me is the idea of looking from above (yes the helicopter again!!!) thus preventing getting bogged down in the detail that the above kind of research will perhaps throw up. [6]
The analysis of the industry that I put up as a starter (see my strategic positioning table in my message of 20th May) I think combines well with Arnold's comments. . . ie the industry participants are moving out of the middle of the table into one extreme or another and are specializing with brands and concepts etc. . . [7]
Maybe some comments on my table, coupled with Arnold's observations, will get some momentum??? [6]
Surely if we can agree that the table provides the scope of what we are looking at then we can really move forward apace??? [7]
   Meredith

IU I June

Meredith I think you are correct in that we need to take a helicopter view. [7]

But I have very little understanding of the industry and so I need a little statistical info to help me consider the total market. [3] Is it growing, shrinking, etc? [2] I live in a rural part of Scotland and so the nearest library that will have a copy of Keynote or Mintel will be over 200 miles away. I can find very little statistical info on the Web. [3] I am happy to discuss the wider issues with you too. [1]

Should we start here, maybe others will agree or disagree with our thoughts?
[7]
As a starter I think the UK market has three/four brewers who control
90%. In the past they have controlled a high percentage of outlets whether
by ownership of pubs, managed houses, tenancies and loans. Hence the Beer
Order to break up this dominance. [4]
In recent years consumption in pubs etc, the Trade has been in decline, due
to drink driving, health issue, change in social habits. In Germany 151 litres
per head of population were consumed in 1976 down to 132 in 1996. [4]
What are the figures for UK I wonder. [2] With a greater swing to beer
purchases from Supermarkets brewers have moved position to being more
in the leisure industry, satisfying the total leisure needs of consumers. Restau-
rants, hotels, holiday camps have all been good sources of profit and cush-
ioned big players from decline in profits from beer. [4]
Maybe they saw that consumption would decline and there would be over
capacity and it would take some time for total production to balance with
consumption. [5]
I wonder if it will in the next 10 years, as over-capacity exists in European
countries due to decline in consumption, see figures on Germany above. [5]
Yours and anyone else's comments would be appreciated. [1]
   Ivan

MW 1 June

   Ivan

Re 'Is this why companies appear in certain spaces on your table?' [1]
I think you are exactly right. [7] because the industry is becoming fragmented
and big players specialising, the smaller players have to take a more focused
position. [8]
(Enforced strategy??)... [6]
IMHO the answer to the TUTOR MARKED ASSIGNMENT questions could
be hung on a discussion such as yours as to why players are moving in the
directions on the table that they are... and what this means for strategies
to the players in the various segments... [8] Any comments anyone?? [1]
Meredith

MH 1 June

   Ivan and Meredith

To quote Grant pp 89–91, in the course book, Industry is an artificial
construct; therefore it is necessary to define what is meant by the Brewing
and pubs as an industry before taking a helicopter view. [6]

> Meredith's 3X3 grid was a great help to me but the surrounding environment needs looking at I believe. [7]
> Nobody has considered the amount of beer that enters the market through supermarkets and the like, as home drinking must be a (poor) substitute for the pub. [6] Also cider and spirits are substitutes for beer both in the pub and at home. [6]
>   Matt

AK 1 June

>   Re: supermarkets.
>
> This is an interesting area. . . [6] Maybe it would help you to ask what do substitutes do. . . [7]
> They create a new industry at the expense of an old industry. . . as well as supermarkets there is the need to think about the effect of cross channel 'smuggling'. . . are these substitutes? [7]
> What do you think?
>   Regards, Andreas [6]

Nearly all the participants responded to the e-moderator's suggestion in this message. They then spent around another 10 days (and 50 messages) relating the sharing of their knowledge to concepts and theories in the course material. All successfully completed and submitted their assignments.

Example 3

Finally, have a look at this example of knowledge construction through interactive CMC in the Information Technology Sector of the same course. There were 11 participants in this conference. The e-moderator was BS, but he didn't intervene during these exchanges. AT (a student) recognizes the need to build a virtual team from the beginning and proposes a group 'mission statement' to get them started. The sequence ended with thanks and an apology from a 'browser'.

AT 19 April

> If we rush into industry analysis too quickly we risk lack of focus. I think we still have work to do in defining the scope. [6]
> 'Mobile communications' could be further divided into the system providers (Orange, Mercury, Vodaphone, Cellnet etc) and customer equipment providers (Nokia, Ericsson, Motorola etc) plus the one stop shop businesses offering equipment and connection services. [7]

Should we address all of these sub-sectors or just one of them? [6]
My inclination is to address only the customer equipment provision sector. [5]
To give us a point of reference for the rest of the conference and the assignment, I think we need a mission statement. Here's my proposal: [7]

> 'The aim of this ITEC2 CMC conference is to analyze and research the attractiveness of the mobile communications customer equipment sector within Europe, evaluate potential strategies to compete within it and assess the sustainability of any strategic advantage. The Objective is to reach a reasoned consensus, within 9 weeks, that will form the basis of a report to the board of an international company entering the sector without infringing the TUTOR MARKED ASSIGNMENT submission rules, with regard to individual work.' [7]

Please feel free to amend, add, and delete etc. so we all know where the goalposts are. I suggest this statement be FROZEN ON 27th APRIL. [7]
Andrew.

JS 20 April

I agree with Andrew that we don't want to get into the analysis before we have agreed a scope. I also agree that we should freeze the objective by 27th April. [6]
However, I would like to add my view to the definition of scope. [6]
There is a further breakdown into Service providers eg Talkland who resell access to Vodaphone, Cellnet, etc. [7]
This may be a more interesting avenue of approach than equipment supply as they have the first line contact with the customers. They have to deal with the issues of churn and customer retention segmentation etc. [6]
Is there anyone else out there who might be interested in this area? [6]
Given that there are 81 people online interested in mobile telecommunications can we cover the three segments and give us all more of a chance to learn about different areas? [6]
Will be away until next week but will be interested in reading your comments when I return. [3]
Jamie

Considerable discussion ensued about the focus on their analysis. At this point, AT attempted a summary:

AT 24 April

Three interest groups seem to be emerging: [7]
Mobile Comms (data and voice)
Internet Services
Communications service provision
Revised Mission statement: [8]
'The aim of this IT CMC conference is to analyze and research the attractive-
ness of the mobile multimedia service provision sector within Europe. This
includes access to and delivery of voice, data, Internet and future multimedia
services by a variety of mobile communications technologies. The conference
will evaluate potential strategies to compete within this sector and assess
the sustainability of any strategic advantage. The Objective is to reach a
reasoned consensus, within 9 weeks, that will form the basis of a report to
the board of an international company entering the sector without infringing
the Tutor Marked Assignment submission rules, with regard to individual
work.' [7]
Comments, counter proposals, hate-mail? [6]
  Andrew

By the agreed date, they had achieved a joint mission. One of the participants
thanked AT for his input:

JS 27 April

Andrew, I would like to echo thanks regarding your input to the Mission
Statement. [6] Afraid I am only just managing to get the time to get
into the Conference but what I have seen regarding the Mission
Statement seems fine by me. [3] Like some others I do not have a
technology background nor do I have any telecomms knowledge so I
will have to rely heavily on those with the appropriate technical
expertise for guidance and help. [3] I now look forward to making
regular visits and input to the Conference. [4] Judith

Resources for practitioners 17

Monitoring e-moderating

You may find it useful to use something like the form below, if you decide to build up monitoring systems for quality assurance in e-moderating. Appoint monitors from experienced e-moderators who can take a collegiate and development approach to supporting and developing others and learn themselves from the experience.

The form can be completed online or in hard copy by the monitor after a visit to a conference.

E-Moderators monitoring report

To: Name of e-moderator   Date: ....

From: Name of Monitor   Copied to: ....

I visited your conference(s) called *(names of conference(s))*

On *(dates and times)*

Here is my reaction to your online activities (as an eavesdropper). Please see my comments as a starting point for a debate. Please contact me by e-mail if you would like to discuss any of them.

Aspects of your e-moderating that seemed to be working well:

eg
I observed that your opening questions were successful because. . .

I noticed that your activity ** went very well because. . .

I thought your review of (assignment, activity, technique) worked really well because . . .

Aspects that I'd like you to reflect on:

eg
Have you tried...

One technique I find helpful is. . .

I noticed that Participant X may need extra help because. . .

Maybe it's time to close off Conference Y because. . .

Here is my personal view on your online activities:

Approach to:	Great	OK	Needs improvement	Comments
Housekeeping				
Use of Time				
Creativity/flexibility				
Content/resources				
Diversity				
Participation				

Best wishes *(name of monitor)*

E-Moderator's response to monitor:

Communicating online

Good online communication cannot simply be directed or taught. Try using these ideas to discuss, change and build on. Eventually when there is some shared agreement, adopt your agreed approach to online communication as a protocol and inform newcomers of the approach from the start.

When to e-mail, when to conference (try this metaphor)

Imagine a conventional pigeonhole system. There is an individual wooden box affixed to the wall for every person in the group, usually with a noticeboard above or nearby too. Now, I have a slip of paper containing information for you. So I pop it in your pigeonhole. However, that information may need to be seen by several people, so I can make copies, and put them in their pigeonhole too. Sometimes, though, the whole group needs to see the information. I can post the message on the noticeboard where everyone can see it in their own time.

Conferencing allows you to do the same thing, only online. You can send a message directly to my individual mailbox, so that only I can see it. It's more secure than if you had put it in a sealed envelope in my physical pigeonhole. Or you can send it to several people at once. Or you can post your message in the conference so that everyone joined to that conference could see it.

The advantage of the pigeonholes and noticeboards being online is that you can use the same method to reply. Everyone else's pigeonhole and noticeboard are right there on your screen.

Use e-mail when:

- You have a message for one or several people that you don't want everyone else to see or they don't need to see.

- The convention is to address messages directly to people who need to take action or who need to reply to you and to copy the messages for information to people who you believe need to know about the content – but think first before sending an unnecessary message!
- The convention is to address messages directly to people who need to take action or reply to you but to 'copy' to people for information only (but only if they need it).

Use conferencing when:

- the message is intended for everyone in a particular group;
- you expect that everyone will have the right to reply;
- there is benefit from everyone in the group seeing replies.

E-communication may be unsuitable when:

- Conveying something upsetting to someone else – choose face-to-face or other synchronous communications.
- To discredit someone by sending e-mail copies to people you consider 'should know' about some problem or misdemeanour. This reflects badly on the sender.
- To perpetuate 'recycling' of a problem or issue without closure or decision. E-mails and conferencing can be very good at exposing and exploring issues. However, someone needs to move to taking and articulating decisions or actions before long.

Online 'netiquette' for e-mails

E-mail conventions:

- Never copy on an e-mail to anyone not on the original list, nor into a conference, without asking and receiving the permission of the originator of the message.
- Be very careful with titles. Choose a short effective title for your e-mail.
- If you reply to someone and change the subject, change the title too.
- Keep to one topic per e-mail with a relevant title. It's far better to send several short e-mails with different titles than one long one covering many subjects.
- If you need to make a number of points in an e-mail, label them 1,2,3. . . This way, it's easy to reply.
- If you reply to just one part of someone else's e-mail, copy and paste their words into the start of your e-mail, so it's clear the sections to which you are referring.
- You can build 'groups' of people to e-mail for your convenience. Use these cautiously and only when your message truly concerns everyone in that group.

If you have frequent messages of that kind, setting up a conference may work better.

- If you receive an e-mail message which has been addressed to a number of people, think carefully before replying to all of them when you may only need to make the comment to the originator of the message, or one or two other people. Some people get very annoyed about many minor e-mails circulating around large groups.
- If you receive a message that contains a 'reply all' to a large group including you, and which you consider irrelevant, simply delete it. Treat it as junk mail. Avoid replying to 'all' again in your anger and perpetuating the problem.

Online 'netiquette' for group conferencing

Enter a CV (résumé) so that others know a little about you. Include:

- something about your background, jobs and interests;
- any particular expertise and support you can offer to others;
- your geographical location.

About computer conferencing conventions:

- Take advantage of training and support to get the most from the computer conferencing software. Then you'll be able to discuss issues rather than ask how to find conferences or send messages. However, you will find people on conferences very willing to help you with anything – just ask.
- The main principles of computer-mediated communication are the same as those of any conversation or dialogue but with a little more emphasis of coming to shared understandings.
- Wide participation without being able to see people offers distinct advantages of any time/any place. It means, however, that you need to be even more considerate than usual in the way you communicate and relate to others online because all communication is text-based and displayed.
- There are delays before response, and with more than a few individuals joined to a conference, considerable complexity results, therefore you need to follow some protocols and conventions.

Communication principles:

- Writing styles tend to be informal.
- Conferences are more public than e-mail, so you need to be careful what you say to or about others.
- Thank, acknowledge and support people freely.
- Acknowledge before differing.
- Speak from your own (or an acknowledged) perspective.

Keeping online communication flowing:

- Lift and quote from the messages of others before replying.
- Use 'emoticons' to convey emotions, eg ☺ to convey a joke.
- Avoid putting words into capital letters – they are considered to be equivalent to shouting.
- Ensure that you place new messages in the appropriate conference.
- Put your test messages in a test conference.
- Put a short effective title for your message.
- When replying to someone else's message, use the same title if the subject remains the same as before, otherwise start a new thread with a new title.
- Keep all messages short – never more than one screenful.
- Use several messages for different topics (this aids replying).
- If you have something longer to say, attach it as a document.

Attaching documents to an e-mail or in a conference message:

- To send or share anything longer than one screenful in a message, it is best to attach a document.
- Make sure the title is clear and there are one or two lines of description in the message so that your recipients can decide whether, and how soon, they need to download the document.
- Make sure that your recipients have suitable software to download and open your document (you may need to make an *.rtf version to be certain).
- Always check a document for viruses, using up-to-date virus checking software, before you send it to others.

Resources for practitioners 19

Valuing online diversity

The skills of relating successfully to the many different kinds of people we encounter through online conferencing are not those any of you reading this book were born with or acquired in childhood. They are however, those that we need to achieve quite quickly in CMC. Those who find this difficult deserve support.

Our message about the value of diversity to trainee e-moderators in the OUBS's online training is reproduced below. Perhaps you can use it as a discussion document with your e-moderators to raise awareness and develop your own protocol?

One of the great strengths of the Open University is the diversity of its students and staff. On management courses in particular, this is a huge educational asset and assists with constructivist approaches. It means we have a uniquely rich variety of backgrounds, perspectives and experience to share and consider. But realizing this potential requires an environment in which people feel able to express what they really think – and, beyond that, to challenge each other and be challenged. This needs to happen in a context of mutual respect, enjoyment and support – a setting where differences as well as similarities are appreciated, and where disagreements are seen as an opportunity to learn, to understand other viewpoints better and to discover the limits of our own beliefs. This can be fun – but it involves risks and can be difficult.

So how do we propose to engineer this learning environment? Alas, there is no way we can ensure it happens – though happily it seems that, in varying degrees, the University does often approximate it. The equal opportunity policy, (which is stated in the student handbook and referred to in the Student Charter), expresses and underpins some of these aspirations. Nevertheless, it would be silly to suggest that we can, somehow, just make happen an honest, challenging and accepting environment.

We suspect that, in the end, the main thing we, as staff, can do is to set the best example we can – and this we will try to. In truth, your own contributions will be of far greater importance. We hope, therefore, that you will join us in trying to establish and maintain a climate in which everyone feels at home, and feels that their contributions are appreciated, even when (indeed, especially when) deep-seated differences are exposed.

Gilly Salmon and Roger Dence.

The challenge to all participants: typing the talk

1. Each conference will develop its own 'cultural' norms. You can set the tone for this by making expectations abundantly clear from the beginning. E-moderators should clarify the conference's purpose and expectations, from the start, and if necessary remind participants from time to time during the conference.
2. When sitting at your keyboard, you may experience the illusion of isolation and safety, similar to that you may feel when driving your car. An e-mail message can then seem like an intrusion. If you are in a CMC conference with others who are expressing views with which you cannot agree, that can be difficult too, but the conference is a more public forum, like being in a train or a plane where you and the other travellers recognize some basic behavioural rules.
3. Views expressed in text messages lack the non-verbal clues, such as facial expression, that add to our face-to-face conversations. This sometimes results in meanings being misinterpreted. Take care therefore with using irony and humour in case they are taken literally. Take account of this when reading the messages of others.
4. If someone accuses others of some incompetence or misdemeanour, there is a strong temptation to play the game of 'Yes! Me too!', 'Ain't it awful!' and 'What's more. . .!' without considering the impact of accumulative accusations. This can create electronic bandwagons. Avoid doing this yourself, and take action against it very fast if you are the e-moderator.
5. Use a short period of 'reflection' before responding immediately to a message that disturbs or upsets you, or even those with which you agree particularly strongly.
6. It's great to pursue minority interests, complaints or opportunities with others online, and if appropriate to enable data collection and take action. However, avoid doing this in the middle of wide interest social or learning conferences. It's best to set up a conference for the purpose to which participants can migrate it they wish.
7. It's rarely necessary to deprive someone of access to the conference because of inappropriate behaviour. However, this can happen if it's clearly in the interests of the majority.

Resources for practitioners 20

A future scenario

How can we prepare people to work as e-moderators in the future? What kind of additional skills will they need? Try putting up this scenario for online discussion by e-moderators, e-mentors and e-trainers. In it, a manager working in the fashion industry, 5 years from now, recalls his day.

London, 12 June

I logged on first thing to get a weather forecast for our area of North London and found that a fine warm day was ahead of us. As always on Fridays, I stayed at Lauren's nursery school for the first hour of the morning. I helped Lauren and the other 3-year-olds with their keyboard skills and onscreen word recognition. I discussed with Mrs Barnes, the play leader, whether Lauren should now move onto a full-size keyboard and whether her vocabulary and clarity of speech were sufficiently developed to start to use voice recognition software.

I decided to sit in the park on the way home and work. The first 250 e-mails took me 55 minutes to deal with. My new colour coding prioritizing software is successful though it had failed to convert some of the German titles properly into English again. I guess it's up to me to learn to programme it a bit better! I was pleased to see that this month's terrestrial meeting in Paris has been transferred to online again – I prefer to avoid that train to Heathrow whenever I can, although I'm still a little curious to see what my new director looks like. I e-mailed her and asked for a video profile. I ordered a pizza delivery, too. I enjoyed a few minutes laughing at the Pizza Zoo's new Web site "My Personal Pizza". It tried to persuade me I could smell the pizza as I saw it cooking but of course I couldn't! It arrived at the door just as I got home.

While eating, I logged into the global customer focus group who are test-wearing the current collection. It's my turn this month to e-moderate this conference. Their main suggestion is for small Velcro pockets in the lightweight Northern Hemisphere trousers to accommodate safely any form of multi-function electronic communicator. I summarized the discussion and e-mailed it to our designers. I downloaded a multi-media 'Happy Birthday' card from my granny: she's never got used to not allowing time for the post (my birthday is tomorrow). I enjoyed the e-collage she had created of my last 10 birthday parties. It's a good thing she wasn't present at one or two I've had! I quickly ordered the weekend shopping at the e-supermarket.

The CrossPond synchronous video meeting with our US partners started at 14.00 GMT. Steve, Jasmine and Andrew were looking very relaxed at breakfast by the ocean in San Diego, despite their early start! The agenda was somewhat dominated by the extent to which the new Internet domain names would be sufficient protection when launching our August interactive leisurewear catalogue. I felt annoyed with Andrew who always aggressively insists that using flowered printed fabric is not a unisex approach. I quickly e-mailed my mentor out of range of the video screen to get ideas on how to avoid conflict with Andrew in future. However, the collection looks great and will appeal to our customers throughout the Western world. Some additional red and yellow colour ranges are being added on the advice of our Beijing partners.

I am using the development of the promotional campaign for the August collection as a case study for my marketing assignment on my MBA. My collaborative learning group is very interested and supportive. The group's comparison with their experiences of promoting products such as books in Africa, medical services in the United States and railway travel in Australia is very instructive and useful. We still have so much to learn about global marketing. I wish that we had useful research and conceptual models to guide us. Our joint assignment on managing people transport networks is coming along well. Fortunately we're a well-balanced group in terms of collaborative and development skills. There're marks for group processes as well as content in the final satellite link presentation.

At 17.30 there was time for my exercise and fitness programme before leaving to collect Lauren. The digital TV carefully tracks my small progress towards greater physical and mental fitness along with a 'Just in Time and Just Enough' aerobics and mind-games video. I'm feeling more alert and energetic! I downloaded a preview of tonight's movies at the same time and printed out the family's weekend diary. Call me old-fashioned, but I like all the appointments stuck up on the fridge!

Resources for practitioners 21

Exploring CMC on the World Wide Web

It is interesting to explore Web sites related to CMC for teaching and learning, and I have given you some suggestions as a start. By the time you read this book, a few may have become obsolete. You may still be able to reach the organization or institution that is listed, however, simply by cutting off the tail of the URL if it happens to be a long one, or by using a search engine.

The Web site for this book is http://oubs.open.ac.uk/e-moderating. I'll endeavour to keep the links up to date on there.

Online journals about CMC

http://www.december.com/cmc/study/center.html is part of John December's US Company. You'll find details of books and other information sources about CMC, plus the now-defunct online *CMC Magazine*. However, there are five years worth of interesting back issues of the *CMC Magazine* available free.

http://www.aln.org is the site of the online *Journal of Asynchronous Learning Networks*, based at Vanderbilt University in the United States. You can also access online the *JALN Magazine*.

http://www.ascusc.org/jcmc is the *Journal of Computer-Mediated Communication*, based at the Annenberg School for Communication at the University of Southern California.

http://www.uwex.edu/disted is the Distance Education Clearinghouse of the University of Wisconsin. Look at DESIEN, the online newsletter.

http://www1.nks.no/eurodl/eurodlen/index.html is the *European Journal of Open and Distance Learning,* available free and online only. You can subscribe to be notified about new articles. The papers include a range on Information and Communication Technologies including CMC, which are available in French and German as well as English.

http://www-jime.open.ac.uk is an online journal about online media in education. Some articles include interactive elements, illustrations and live electronic links. The journal uses open CMC to conduct its article review processes.

http://jan.ucc.nau.edu/~ipct-j is another online journal about CMC, reviewed, easily accessed, regularly updated and searchable journal with most contributors and editorial from the United States.

http://www.techknowlogia.org is a newish, free online journal for 'policy makers, strategists, practitioners and technologists'. I like the way the site works and the journal has wide international coverage.

Find a Virtual Campus?

http://www.insead.fr/calt takes you to the Centre for Advanced Learning Technologies at INSEAD, a leading French college for management education. Have a look at the Centre's Virtual Worlds: instructions are provided for downloading the software needed.

http://www.adm.monash.edu.au/ched/courses/GCHE/index.html is the page for looking at Monash University's (based in Melbourne, Australia) Graduate Certificate in Higher Education. You can try a demonstration of the CMC software that they use, InterLearn.

http://www.shu.ac.uk/virtual_campus takes you to the welcome page for the Virtual Campus of Sheffield Hallam University. You will see that for certain courses it is possible to study at a distance, with support provided at least in part through e-mail and/or conferencing in FirstClass or TopClass.

http://www.wgu.edu is the website for Western Governors University, a virtual university located in Salt Lake City. It is virtual in the sense that it is a broker for online courses offered by other US institutions.

http://www.cvc.edu takes you into the California Virtual Campus, which is a link page taking you to courses and services offered by Californian universities and colleges. Have a look at a few of them and you'll find they vary widely in the extent to which they are online.

http://www.cuonline.edu is the online campus of the University of Colorado. The welcome page says that for more than a hundred courses students can interact with their instructors and fellow-students using e-mail and bulletin boards.

http://iet.open.ac.uk takes you to the online Postgraduate Qualifications in Open and Distance Education programme of the Institute of Educational Technology at the Open University. You can reach a Virtual Campus page, but access to the 'rooms' for students is only by password.

http://www.geteducated.com enables you to obtain the online *Virtual University Gazette* and you can read the lists of North American institutions offering distance learning. The site belongs to Geteducated.com, a US consultancy group.

http://www.regents.edu is the site for Regents College, which claims to be the United States' first virtual university.

http://www.fsu.edu/~distance takes you to the Office of Distributed and Distance Learning at Florida State University in Tallahassee. Have a look at the open and distance learning option, which includes CMC, in the Graduate Programs. Likewise the criminology option.

http://database.telecampus.com is the online course directory of TeleCampus, based in Canada.

http://www.unext.com is the site of a US company, based in Illinois, intending to market advanced university-level courses with Internet support. Watch this space!

http://stanford-online.stanford.edu tells you about Stanford Online, part of Stanford University's Professional Development Program. Video, audio, text and graphics are used to deliver course material.

http://oubs.open.ac.uk takes you into the Open University's Business School. Only registered students and staff can enter the CMC sites.

http://www.uophx.edu is the University of Phoenix – which has sparked off interest and comment because of its success as a for-profit institution. Some courses teach and learn online and its instructors receive training in CMC. You can read an article about it in TechKnowLogia (Jackson, 2000).

Online databases

http://www-icdl.open.ac.uk is a useful searchable and browsable database for published research and open and distance learning courses. The database shows over 33,000 open and distance learning courses. Online courses are growing fast though it is hard to tell how many of them have good interaction or e-moderating.

http://www.kn.pacbell.com/wired/bluewebn is a searchable database of about 1000 outstanding school-oriented Internet learning sites, particularly those with online activities. Providers range from museums to companies.

Software for CMC

http://collaborate.shef.ac.uk/resources.html is the site for Sheffield University's commentary on a wide variety of CMC resources and software, with illustrative links so you can try out the 'look and feel' of software. This is especially worthwhile for those looking for overview and comparisons between widely available software and examples of use.

http://www.softarc.com is the site for FirstClass, the CMC system used widely in the Open University's courses.

http://www.wbtsystems.comis is the site for TopClass, another CMC system, made by a company in the United States.

http://www.lotus.com is the developer's site for Lotus Notes and http://www.lotus.com/home.nsf/welcome/stories is Lotus' success stories. These include academic and training examples of its use.

http://www.lotus.com/home.nsf/tabs/learnspace is the developer's site for Lotus Learning Space which combines asynchronous and synchronous conferencing with other facilities such as authoring tools.

http://www.ualberta.ca/WEBCT is the supplier's site for Web CT. By following links on this page, you can read some reviews and advice about its use from the University of Alberta.

http://hyperserver.engrg.uwo.ca/magy2 is a Canadian example of a Web environment for collaborative working. The SunStang is a solar-driven motor car and engineers are invited to contribute to its further development.

http://www.umuc.edu is the Web site of the University of Maryland's University College, just outside Washington DC. WebTycho is worth looking at: it's a CMC system, complete with online training of students.

Resources for practitioners 22

What will we call ourselves?

Many educators now talk about the 'Guide on the Side' rather than the 'Sage on the Stage' to indicate more facilitative approaches to teaching. We need to update this image for e-moderators to reflect the need for electronic conferencing experience.

I suggest you use this list for workshops and online discussion with e-moderators to explore the role in your context.

1. **E-moderator:** I've chosen this term to refer to online teaching and facilitation roles. The term moderator has grown up with CMC and has been used from the earliest days for online conference facilitators. Moderating used to mean to preside over a meeting or discussion. I have added the 'e' short for electronic to the front of it, borrowed from e-commerce and e-mail, to indicate the wider and special responsibilities that the online context adds to the role. Zane Berge in North America and myself in Europe appear to have started using the term e-moderator at much the same time, as the millennium turned. Zane Berge and Mauri Collins maintain a useful and popular e-moderators page that can be found at:
http://www.emoderators.com/moderators.shtml

2. **Online negotiator:** where knowledge construction online is desired, the key role for the e-moderator is one of negotiating the meaning of activities and information through online discussion and construction.

3. **Online host:** since the social role of online working is important, you may want to have a social host (or hostess) as well as e-moderators for the teaching and learning conferences. They do not need to run social events online as such (though they may) but ensure everyone is greeted and introduced to others with like-minded interests.

4. **Personal learning trainer:** this is a suggestion from Robin Mason. Learners may need a personal trainer to lead them through materials and networks, identify relevant materials and advisors and ways forward (Mason, 1998).

5. **Convenor** is a term that we've adopted in the OUBS and have used especially for online conferences and courses where there is a fairly wide audience. The Business Café conferences associated with a network TV programme provide an example: http://oubs.open.ac.uk/businesscafe

6. **Online conductor:** this suggests the pulling together of a variety of resources as people (as in conducting an orchestra to produce a beautiful integrated sound) or perhaps electrical current conductors – if your conferences are effective and flow along, there will be energy, excitement and power!

7. **Online concierge:** to provide support and information on request (perhaps a map of the area. . .).

8. **Online manager:** much of e-moderating is also 'managing', especially in its up-to-date definition of coaching, supporting and leading. Managerial roles in conferencing include developing objectives, agendas, timetables, rules and group norms. Managing the interactions and capacity of a group is a key success factor in e-moderating, as in management.

9. **E-Police:** I hope you will not call yourself this, nor find the need to make laws and enforce them. You will of course need a Code of Practice and protocols for e-moderators.

10. **Online Chair:** an E-chair would be useful if a structured meeting with clear action outcomes is needed. The skills of chairing online are similar to those of chairing a face-to-face meeting, with the added complexity and asynchronicity, that should result in more democratic decision-taking and hence more time than usual.

11. **Online leader:** this is a term I've not seen used. I expect this is because CMC tends to be a highly democratic medium and leadership may not be seen as quite appropriate. However, e-moderators are truly leaders – they need to set objectives and processes and provide and maintain optimum conditions online for the realization of these.

12. **E-teacher:** the terms 'teacher', 'trainer' and 'tutor' are generic and have the advantage of being in common use. Therefore adding 'e-' in front of them to indicate the electronic element probably makes them acceptable in most online courses and processes. I think the term then suggests a more facilitative and developmental role than traditional teaching.

13. **E-Master:** The term master has come into use in recent years in terms of 'Web-Master' – someone who takes a particular responsibility for the technical, design and perhaps the editorial content of a Web site. The notion of CMC 'Master' could be introduced meaning the sporting term of 'master', ie someone who has previously won a number of games.

14. **Faceless Facilitator:** this is a suggestion from Tan Lay In of Ngee Ann Polytechnic, Singapore. She reminds us that considerable skill change is needed in instructors experienced in face-to-face facilitation in order to promote online collaboration. (Tan, 1999).

15. **Tele-coach or tele-tutor:** from Germany comes a reminder that learning free of space and time needs a tele-coach (as opposed to a 'presence' coach) able to support learners into the new paradigms in the way coaches used to by being physically beside trainees (Mundemann, 1999).

16. **Online Gardener:** this is an idea from the corporate training sector. E-moderators not only need to 'cultivate the garden' (by helping learners acquire knowledge) but also make the garden grow (by increasing the store of knowledge available) (Benque, 1999).

17. Try these metaphors out in discussion in your e-moderator training: E-Ringmaster, Online priest, Agent provocateur, Devil's advocate.

References

Agre, P E and Rotenberg, M (1997) *Technology and Privacy,* MIT Press, Cambridge MA

Bacsich, P and Ash, C (1999) *The Hidden Costs of Networked Learning in UK Universities,* Proceedings of Online Educa, Berlin

Bakia, M (2000) Costs of ICT use in higher education: what little we know, *TechKnowLogia* **2** (1) pp http://www.techknowlogia.org

Benjamin, A (1994) Affordable, restructured education: a solution through information technology, *RSA Journal,* (May), pp 45–9

Benque, N (1999) *Online Training for Tutors,* Proceedings of Online Educa, Berlin

Bevan, E (1999) personal e-mail: 22nd December

Biggs, J (1995) The role of metalearning in study processes, *British Journal of Educational Psychology* **55,** pp 185–212

Billett, S (1996) Towards a model of workplace learning; the learning curriculum, *Studies in Continuing Education* **15** (1) pp 43–57

Blumer, H (1969) *Symbolic Interaction,* Prentice-Hall, Englewood Cliffs, NJ

Brown, S (1998) Reinventing the university, *Association for Learning Technology Journal* **6** (3), pp 30–7

Brown, S, Bull, J and Race, P (1999) *Computer Assisted Assessment in Higher Education,* Kogan Page, London

Bruner, J (1986) The language of education, in *Actual Minds, Possible Worlds,* ed J Bruner, Harvard University Press, Cambridge, MA

Cann, A J and Pawley, E L (1999) Automated online tutorials: new formats for assessment on the WWW, in *Computer-Assisted Assessment in Higher Education,* eds S Brown, J Bull and P Race, Kogan Page, London

Chenault, B G (1998) Developing personal and emotional relationships via computer-mediated communication, *CMC Magazine* **5** (5): http://www.december.com/cmc/mag/1998/may/toc.html

Debenham, M D, Whitelock, M, Fung, P and Emms, JM (1999) Online educational counselling for students with special needs: building rapport, *Association for Learning Technology Journal,* **7** (1) pp 19–25

Dence, R D (1996) *Reviewing Conference Discussions On Participation And Contribution: Lurking or differently active?,* report for Institute of Educational Technology, OU, Milton Keynes: January

DiPaolo, A (1999) *Online education: Myth or reality? The Stanford Online Experience,* Proceedings of Online Educa, Berlin

DiPaolo, A (2000) Personal telephone conversation, 11th January

Duchastel, P (1997) A Web-based model for university instruction, *Journal of Educational Technology Systems,* **25** (3) pp 221–8

Eden, C (1990) Working on problems using cognitive mapping, in *Operations Research in Management,* eds S C Littlechild and M Shutler, Prentice Hall, London

Eden, C, Ackermann, F and Cropper, S (1992) The analysis of cause maps, *Journal of Management Studies,* **3** (29), pp 309–24

Feenberg, A (1989) The written word, in *Mindweave, Communication, Computers & Distance Education,* eds R D Mason and A R Kaye, Pergamon, Oxford

Gold, J (1998) Disability and CMC, *Computer Mediated Communications Magazine* **5** (1) : 1 http://www.december.com/cmc/mag/1998/jan/toc.html

Gray, C and Salmon, G (1999) Academic integrity in electronic universities of the new millennium: a practioner's perspective, *Higher Education in Europe,* **XXIV** (2), pp 259–64

Haddad, W D (2000) Higher education: the ivory tower and the satellite dish, *TechKnow-Logia,* **2** (1): www.techknowlogia.org

Halliday, M A K and Hasan, R (1989) *Language, Context and Text: Aspects of Language in a Social-semiotic Perspective,* Oxford University Press, Oxford

Hawkridge, D (1998) Cost-effective support for university students learning via the Web?, *Association for Learning Technology Journal,* **6** (3), pp 25–9

Hawkridge, D, Morgan, A and Jelfs, A (1997) *H801 Students' and Tutors' Use of the Electronic Workbook and Electronic Mail 1997,* OU Report to the Electronic Tutoring Group, Milton Keynes, December

Hendry, G (1996) Constructivism and educational practice. *Australian Journal of Education,* **40** (1), pp 19–45

Henri, F (1992) Computer conferencing and content analysis, in *Collaborative Learning Through Computer Conferencing: The Najaden Papers,* ed A Kaye, Springer-Verlag, Heidelberg

Holsti, O R (1968) Content analysis, in *The Handbook of Social Psychology: Research methods,* eds G Lindzey and E Aronson, Addison-Wesley, Reading, MA

Honey, P and Mumford, A (1986) *Using Your Learning Styles,* Honey, Maidenhead

Jackson, G B (2000) A new model for tertiary education in developing countries?, *TechKnowLogia* **2** (1) :http://www.techknowlogia.org

Jennings, C (1999) personal e-mail, 19 December

Jewett, F I (1999) *BRIDGE: A simulation model for comparing the costs of expanding a campus using distributed instruction versus classroom instruction,* Proceedings of Online Educa, Berlin

Jonassen, D, Davidson, M, Collins, M, Campbell, C and Haag, B B (1995) Constructivism and computer-mediated communication in distance education, *American Journal of Distance Education* **9** (2), pp 7–25

Kelly, G A (1955) *The Psychology of Personal Constructs,* Norton, New York

Lapham, C (1998) A mindset for the new millennium, *CMC Magazine,* **5** (10) : http://www.december.com/cmc/mag/1998/oct/lapnp.html

Latchem, C and Lockwood, F (eds) (1998) *Staff Development in Open and Flexible Learning,* Routledge, London

Leach, J and Moon, B (1999) Recreating pedagogy, in *Learners and Pedagogy,* eds J Leach and B Moon, Paul Chapman, London

Leino, A (1999) *Virtual United: Online course to 22 countries by an international team,* Proceedings of Online Educa, Berlin

Loknes, R L (2000) personal telephone conversation, 11 January

Mason, R (1993) Written interactions, in *Computer Conferencing, The last word*, ed R. Mason, pp 3–19, Beach Holme, Victoria, British Colombia

Mason, R (1998) *Globalising Education: Trends and applications*, Routledge, London

Masterton, S (1998) The virtual participant: a tutor's assistant for electronic conferencing, in *Knowledge Web*, eds M Eisenstadt and T Vincent, Kogan Page, London

Moran, L (1997) Flexible learning as university policy, in *Open and Distance Learning in Industry and Education*, ed S Brown, Kogan Page, London

Morgan, D L (1988) *Focus Groups as Qualitative Research*, Sage, Beverley Hills, CA

Mundemann, F (1999) *Certified Training for Tele-coaches*, Proceedings of Online Educa, Berlin

Murphy, D (1999) *Still 'getting the mixture right': Increasing interaction on the Internet*, Proceedings of 8th Conference on Open and Distance Learning, 'Learning and Teaching with New Technologies', Cambridge, UK, 28 Sept–1 Oct

Newell, A (1999) Enabling technologies, *The Times Higher Educational Supplement*, p 13, 16 April

Norman, D (1999) *The Invisible Computer*, MIT Press, Cambridge, MA

O'Reilly, M and Morgan, C (1999) *Assessing Open and Distance Learners*, Kogan Page, London

Potter, J and Wetherell, M (1989) *Discourse and Social Psychology*, Sage, London

Preece, J (1999) Empathic communities: balancing emotional and factual communication, *Interacting With Computers*, **12**, pp 63–77.

Preece, J (2000) *Online Communities: Supporting sociability and designing usability*, John Wiley & Sons, Chichester

Pullen, J M (1998) ClassWise: synchronous Internet desktop education, *http://bacon.gmu.edu/pubs/ClassWise/tr98-06.html* IEEE Transitions in Education

Putman, R W (1991) Recipes and reflective learning: 'What would prevent you from saying it that way?', in *The Reflective Turn: Case studies in and on educational practice*, ed D Schön, Teachers College Press, London and New York

Rheingold, H (1995) *The Virtual Community*, Minerva, London

Robinson, H, Smith, M, Galpin, F, Birchall, D and Turner, I (1998) As good as IT gets: have we reached the limits of what technology can do for us?, *Active Learning*, **9** (December), pp 50–3

Rodine, C R, Kotter, M and Shield, L (1999) *Voice Conferencing on the Internet: Creating richer on-line communities for distance learning*, Proceedings of EdMedia

Rogers, A (1993) Adult learning maps and the teaching process, *Studies in the Education of Adults*, **25** (2) pp 203–6

Rossman, M H (1999) Successful online teaching using asynchronous learning discussion forum, *Asynchronous Learning Networks* **3** (2) : http://www.aln.org/alnweb/journal/jaln-vol3issue2.htm

Rowntree, D (1995) Teaching and learning online: a correspondence education for the 21st century?, *British Journal of Educational Technolog, y* **26** (3), pp 205–15

Rumble, G (1997) *The Costs and Economics of Open and Distance Education*, Kogan Page, London

Rumble, G (1999) *The Costs of Networked Learning: What have we learnt?* Proceedings of Flexible Learning on the Information Superhighway (FLISH), Sheffield, http://www.shu.ac.uk/flish/choice.htm

Salmon, G (1998a) Developing learning though effective online moderation, *Active Learning*, **9** (December), pp 3–8

Salmon, G (1998b) *Student Induction and Study Preparation Online*, Proceedings of Networks of Skills and Competence: Telematics in Education, Joensuu, Finland, September

Salmon, G (1999a) Computer mediated conferencing in large scale management education, *Open Learning,* (June), pp 45–54

Salmon, G (1999b) *Managers of the Future,* http://www.open.ac.uk/businesscafe Business Briefing for the Business Cafe TV series 25.4.99

Salmon, G (2000) Computer mediated conferencing for management learning at the Open University, *Management Learning,* forthcoming

Santoro, G P (1995) What is computer-mediated communication?, in *Computer-mediated Communication and the Online Classroom,* eds ZL Berge and MP Collins, pp 11–27, Hampton Press, NJ

Schön, D (1983) *The Reflective Practitioner: How professionals think in action,* Basic Books, London

Schreiber, D A and Berge, Z L (eds) (1998) *Distance Training: how innovative organizations are using technology to maximize learning and meet business objectives,* Jossey-Bass Inc, California

Scott, P and Eisenstadt, M (1998) Exploring telepresence on the Internet: the KMI Stadium Webcast experience, in *The Knowledge Web,* eds M Eisenstadt and T Vincent, Kogan Page, London

Selinger, M and Pearson, J (eds) (1999) *Telematics in Education: Trends and Issues,* Elsevier, Oxford

Semaan, S (2000) Speech recognition: when people talk, computer listen, *TechKnowLogia,* **2** (1) : http://www.techknowlogia.org

Spender, D (1995) *Nattering on the Net,* Spinifex Press, North Melbourne

Spender, D (1999) Personal e-mail:, 17 December

Steeples, C, Vincent, P and Chapman, G (1997) *The Internet as a Collaborative Learning Resource,* CSALT, Teaching Developments Database, Lancaster

Stenhouse, L (1975) *Introduction to Curriculum Research and Development,* Heinemann, London

Stewart, T (1997) *Intellectual Capital,* Nicholas Brealey, London

Susman, M (1999) The Virtual Reality Campus: reality check for the 21st century, *Journal of Telecommunication in Higher Education,* 3 (Fall), pp 24–7

Tan, L (1999) *The 'Faceless Facilitator': An impossible learning approach?,* Proceedings of Online Educa, Berlin

Tiffin, J and Rajasingham, L (1997) *In Search of the Virtual Class: Education in an information society,* Routledge, London

Van Grundy, A B (1988) *Techniques of Structured Problem Solving,* Van Nostrand Reinhold, New York

Vygotsky, L S (1978) *Mind in Society,* Harvard University Press, Cambridge, MA

Young, G and Marks-Maran, D (1999) A case study of convergence between conventional and distance education, in *The Convergence of Conventional and Distance Education,* eds A Tait and R Mills, Routledge, New York

Index